On the Pa

An Illustrated Source Book on the Care of the Poor
under the Old Poor Law

Based on Documents from the County of Glamorgan

by

Raymond K. J. Grant, B.A., Ph.D.
of the Middle Temple
Barrister-at-Law

A Glamorgan Archive Service Publication

1 Scotch Beggars, watercolour by George Delamotte, *c*.1819.

CONTENTS

The said Examinant saith that he was born some where near Cork in the
Kingdom of Ireland, that his Father was an American & he was carr[y]d
Philadelphia when he was young, & that he served an apprenticesh[ip]
Board a Ship belonging to one Mr Joseph Pemberton a merchant in Phi[la]
dolphia, that about 13 or 14 years ago he was prest at Halifax in No[rth]
America on Board the Foresane Captn Spry, that about 12 years ag[o]
was turn'd over to the Terrible Captn Collins, that about 13 years a[go]
was turn'd over at Woolwich to the now Thunder Captn Proby, & Sail'd
Mediterranean, that in reefing the Main top Sail, one of the reef Poi[nts]
him on the left Eye, wch he lost, And the anguish & Pain of that blinded
right Eye, he was then sent home to Portsmouth in the Wager a twenty
Ship, but who was the Captn of her, he has forgot, And that the Fleet in
Mediterranean was then Commanded by Admiral Saunders; that he wa[s]
off at Portsmouth & turn'd Adrift, that he then sent to his wife who [?]
lived at Honiton in Devonshire, & whose maiden name was Deborah B[?]
And married to him abt 15 years ago in Stonehouse Church between
Plymouth and York, that since his discharge at Portsmouth he has tra[velled]
about, that in Towns he is lead by a Dog & begs and his wife sells gar[ters]
Garters & other trifling things without any Licence, and he has continued
until he was taken up this day in the Town of Swansea as he was begging
Street.

the mark of

Sworn at Swansea in the
sd County. before me
Gab. Powell

alexander ⊢ Culbert

2   Swansea. The examination of a blind beggar, 1772.

FOREWORD

The study of history from the sources is a stimulating experience and gives a new dimension to the subject. We can thereby examine the impact of general trends and movements upon the individual lives of ordinary men and women; this approach sharpens our awareness that history is a human study—that it is primarily about people. When case studies are selected from local records, the familiar setting gives the story additional relevance and significance for the reader; local history nurtures the parallel concepts of continuity and change in human affairs.

A source book with this purpose was made by Dr. Grant in his *Parliamentary History of Glamorgan* (Christopher Davies, 1978),covering the period 1542–1976. The present volume seeks to do the same for the Old Poor Law in Glamorgan down to 1834; the wealth of human interest in the documents makes the subject, I believe, especially suitable for this kind of treatment.

Both the *Parliamentary History of Glamorgan* and the present volume have their origin in courses organised for sixth-form History students by the Glamorgan Education Committee at its residential Educational Centre at Duffryn House, St. Nicholas, from 1955 until 1979. Close co-operation between Dr. Grant and the Record Office enabled students to study selected original documents from the county archives. Since these early beginnings, further systematic research by Dr. Grant has resulted in the present volume.

Patricia Moore
Glamorgan Archivist

ACKNOWLEDGEMENTS

The author wishes to make grateful acknowledgement of the co-operation of the Glamorgan Archivist, Mrs. Patricia Moore, BA, FSA, and her staff. The source material used in this book is drawn mainly from the records in the Glamorgan Record Office. Mrs. Moore has at all times given invaluable assistance in making these records available for study, in suggesting additional material, in procuring facsimile documents and illustrations of the high quality required, and in all the time-consuming technical details involved in preparing a source book of this kind for publication. The book itself appears as one of a long series of important publications on Glamorgan history which have appeared under the auspices of the Glamorgan Archives Joint Committee.

The National Library of Wales is to be thanked for permission to reproduce the watercolours of characters from the Swansea area painted by George Delamotte. Dover Publications Inc. of New York earn warm thanks for their liberal attitude to the reproduction of their facsimile publications.

The main cost of the volume has been borne by the Glamorgan Archive Service, but acknowledgement is also made of the substantial financial assistance and support for the publication of this book generously given by the Chairman and members of the Education Committee of the Mid Glamorgan County Council. They, and the Director of Education, have shown active encouragement for projects to introduce local history to students and to the general public.

Unless otherwise indicated, all documents cited are in the care of the Glamorgan Archive Service. They fall into four main categories:

Parish Records

1. *Vestry Minute books.*

The more substantial ratepayers in the parish met periodically at the parish Vestry meeting. Their decisions on matters concerning the parish church, the relief of paupers, and highway matters were recorded by the parish clerk in a minute book kept for that purpose. Vestry minute books for most of the ancient parishes of Glamorgan (between 120 and 130 in number) for the period before 1834 have been lost, but those for twenty-two parishes survive—twenty in the Glamorgan Record Office, and two in the National Library of Wales, Aberystwyth.

2. *Overseers' Account books.*

Unpaid Overseers of the Poor were appointed from amongst the parishioners. They held office for one year, and with the Churchwardens collected and distributed the poor rate. They had of course to keep accounts. Overseers' accounts for our period survive in the Glamorgan Record Office for forty parishes in the county, and for one other in the National Library of Wales.

Glamorgan Quarter Sessions Records

The Justices of the Peace for Glamorgan county met in Quarter Sessions four times a year, at or about Epiphany (January 6th), Easter, Midsummer (June 24th) and Michaelmas (September 29th). Epiphany Sessions were held at Cardiff, Easter Sessions at Cowbridge, and Midsummer Sessions at Neath. Michaelmas Sessions were held at Cardiff until 1775; after that the increasing importance of Swansea caused them to be held there.

The administrative duties of Quarter Sessions were transferred to County Councils by the Local Government Act of 1888 (51 & 52 Vict. c. 41), and the Court itself was abolished by the Courts Act 1971 (c. 23).

3. *Quarter Sessions Rolls*

The Court of Quarter Sessions, in addition to its other work, dealt with a multitude of Poor Law matters—appeals of all kinds, general regulations, orders regarding individual paupers, and so on. A great number of documents relating to these cases was sent to the Clerk of the Peace, who was the Clerk of the Court, by Justices of the Peace, Overseers of the Poor, High Constables and Petty Constables, the Keeper of the House of Correction and others who had indictments to make and accounts to be rendered. These papers formed the Court's case-list for each Sessions. They were kept together, or 'filed', by being threaded on a long tape, and then rolled up into a bundle; hence the term Quarter Sessions Rolls.

The earliest Glamorgan Quarter Sessions Rolls to survive, preserved in the Record Office, are those for Easter and Midsummer 1727, and for Epiphany 1728. For the period 1729 to 1834 a complete series of rolls for four sessions in each year has survived. In the Record Office catalogue Epiphany Sessions Rolls are marked 'A', Easter Sessions 'B', Midsummer Sessions 'C', and Michaelmas Sessions 'D'.

4. Quarter Sessions Order or Minute Books
The *'Justices of the Peace in Quarter Session assembled'* heard the cases contained in the Rolls produced by the Clerk of the Peace, and then made decisions or orders concerning them. The clerks of the Court recorded the proceedings and the judgements in leather-bound 'Order' or 'Minute' books; many of these cases concerned the Poor Law.

Eighteen Quarter Sessions Order or Minute books are extant for our period. The earliest Order book (GRO Q/S M vol. 1) covers the Sessions from Midsummer 1719 to Michaelmas 1738, and the latest for our period (GRO Q/S M vol. 18) covers those from Easter 1833 to Epiphany 1837.

SURVIVAL OF RECORDS

The documents which have survived, both in the Glamorgan Quarter Sessions collection and from individual parishes, date (with a few rare exceptions) from the eighteenth century and from the early nineteenth century. They cover a period which saw the acceleration of industrial development in the region and the influx of population from outside the county into the expanding industrial and urban areas.

Amongst the surviving records the Vestry minute books from Llantrisant parish constitute an unrivalled source of evidence, and for this reason many of the extracts cited come from this series. Quotations and illustrations from a variety of parishes or hamlets widen the coverage of the subject into the area of the old historic county.

SPELLING AND PUCTUATION

Many words in the original documents are spelt differently from modern usage. In the eighteenth century a limited number of people in each parish would have been able to read and write. The parishioners who made their marks rather than signed their names at the foot of the Vestry minutes give evidence of this. Those who wrote spelled the words as they pronounced them. The eighteenth century saw the compilation of dictionaries such as that of Dr. Johnson, published in 1755, and the English-Welsh dictionary of John Walters which was printed in Cowbridge and appeared in parts between 1770 and 1783. During the nine-teenth century more people became literate. Their reading of books and newspapers, coupled with the publication of an increasing amount of printed material, in which consistency was desirable, led to the widespread adoption of accepted spellings.

In many eighteenth-century documents the word 'the' was written 'ye' (pronounced 'the'), the 'y' representing the sound of the Anglo-Saxon letter 'thorn'. The form 'ye' has been retained in the transcriptions, to aid the eye. The eighteenth-century practice of printing the long 's', which resembled an 'f' without its bar, was also used in a written form, especially for the first of a double 's'. This can be seen, for instance, in the surname Rosser.

Modern punctuation has been added to some transcriptions, in order to make them easier to read. All quotations from documents are set in italics, and within quotation marks.

NOTE ON MONEY

Sums of money in the documents were expressed in the old coinage current before decimalization in 1971. There were 12 pence to the shilling, and 20 shillings to the pound. When written in figures, 1/-, or 1s.0d., for example, represents one shilling, and 2/6, or 2s.6d., two shillings and six pence. A guinea was one pound and one shilling, £1 1s.0d. A fourth column was added to some accounts of pounds, shillings and pence to accommodate a halfpenny, ½d., or farthing, ¼d.

GLOSSARY

Apothecary—In the Middle Ages restricted to those who prepared and sold drugs. By the eighteenth century the term had come to be used of a general medical practitioner, a poor man's physician.

Engross—To write out a legal document in a large fair hand.

High Constable—Constable of a Hundred Division.

Hundred division—A territorial division within a county. See page 74.

Indictment—A formal accusation; the document which contains the charge.

Overseer of the Poor—An official, nominated from amongst the parishioners, to levy a rate and make disbursements towards the care of the poor.

Pass—A document carried by a pauper licensing him to travel from one parish to another.

Petty or Parish Constable—A parish official charged with keeping law and order.

Quorum—A fixed number of members that must be present to make proceedings of an assembly valid. In earlier times, some Justices of the Peace enjoyed a status superior to others. Legal documents were required to be validated by these superior Justices; they were known as Justices 'of the Quorum'. By the eighteenth century, this distinction had disappeared. All Justices of the Peace enjoyed equal legal status within their respective jurisdictions, but the requirement that one of the Justices signing and sealing a legal document must be 'of the Quorum' survived as a meaningless formula.

To wit—An archaic verb meaning to have knowledge of, to know. The first words of certain legal documents.

Vestry—A meeting of the substantial ratepayers of a parish to transact business.

ABBREVIATIONS

alias —otherwise
esq. —esquire
f. —folio
ff. —folios
gent. —gentleman
GRO —Glamorgan Record Office
JP —Justice of the Peace
NLW —National Library of Wales
p. —page
pp. —pages
Q/S M —Quarter Sessions Minute (or Order) books
Q/S R —Quarter Sessions Rolls
Rev. —Reverend
v. —*verso*, the back or dorse.
WGARO —West Glamorgan Area Record Office

LIST OF ILLUSTRATIONS

Most, but not all, documents illustrated have been transcribed in the text.
Page numbers in brackets refer to transcriptions of illustrations.
Some documents are shown smaller than actual size.

20.	40	Llandaff. Extract from Overseer's accounts.	1754	P/53/38
21.	42	Llansannor. A list of a pauper's possessions.	1786	NLW Llansannor parish book
22.	45 (47)	Llandeilo Talybont. Vestry arranges rented poor-house accommodation.	1790	P/108/8 p. 78
23.	46 (46)	Llantrisant. Milk for the parish workhouse.	1785	P/62/4 p. 78
24.	50	Margam. The examination of John Price, a rogue and vagabond found begging.	1770	Q/S R 1770A 93
25.	51	John Lumley, one of Lord Nelson's seamen, watercolour by George Delamotte.	c.1819	NLW vol. 271
26.	54 (53)	Swansea. A magistrate orders the High Constable of Swansea to convey Margaret Carty, a rogue and vagabond, back to Ireland.	1759	Q/S R 1759D 5
27.	56	Bettws. A list of those who brought a Settlement Certificate when they moved into the parish.	1746	P/77/3 p. 125
28.	59	An Irishman going to Cork, watercolour by George Delamotte.	May 1819	NLW vol. 271
29.	63 (63)	Llangynwyd, Cwmdu hamlet. A pauper boarded out.	1815	P/82/13 p. 57
30.	64 (64)	Llangynwyd, Cwmdu hamlet. The 'Roundsman' system.	1811	P/82/13 p. 29

| Back cover | Elizabeth Williams, Llansamlet, watercolour by George Delamotte. | *c.*1819 | NLW vol. 271 |

The watercolours by George Delamotte of characters painted in the Swansea area come from an album of his work in the National Library of Wales. It is entitled 'Costume drawings', reference, vol. 271 quarto.

The line drawings interspersed in the text are taken from *Rustic Vignettes for Artists and Craftsmen, Illustrations from Ackermann's Edition of the 'Microcosm'* by W. H. Pyne, in a facsimile edition published by Dover Publications, Inc., New York, in 1977.

CHAPTER ONE

The Parish Vestry Meeting
The Poor Rate

In Tudor times the government was faced by serious problems at home. The number of unemployed increased; during the Middle Ages the monks had fed the poor daily at their gates, but the closing of the monasteries by Henry VIII put an end to that. The countryside was terrorised by gangs of wandering beggars.

At first Parliament tried to solve the problem by harsh punishments for beggars, such as whipping and branding. But gradually it was realised that there were three kinds of poor people, and each required different treatment. First there were old, sick and disabled people, who needed treatment in hospital, or help to enable them to live in their own homes. Second, there were able-bodied people, willing to work but unable to find it; plans were made to teach them a craft and provide opportunities for work. Third, there were 'incorrigible rogues', able but unwilling to work; these were to be regarded as criminals and punished in various ways.

These objectives were embodied in a series of Tudor Acts of Parliament, culminating in the famous 'Act of Elizabeth' in 1601 (43 Eliz. I. c. 2). These laws made it the duty of each parish to look after its own poor, a duty performed at the meeting of parishioners known as the parish Vestry. The Vestry had since medieval times been responsible for the maintenance and repair of the parish church; it continued to be so until the ancient compulsory church rate was abolished in 1868 (31 & 32 Vict. c. 109). At a meeting held in Llantrisant on 10th November 1786, for example, it was *'Ordered that a Rate of Fourpence in the Pound be raised by the Churchwardens of this Parish for New Leading the Parish Stiple for this Current year'*. (**Llantrisant Vestry minute book**, p. 102).

But Tudor governments had found that they could use this parish Vestry meeting to carry out their local policies; for more than two hundred years afterwards the parish continued to look after the roads and the poor in addition to their original responsibilities. So at Llancarfan on 3rd April 1826 it was *'unanimously agreed by the under signed parshone[r]s in Vestry asembled, that the Churchwardens & Overseers of the poor, are to make a general survey of the whole parish, to make a general Valueation, on purpose of makeing leaugal Rates, for the relief of the poor and other nessisaries, and also Church, and Road Rates'*. This was

I

signed by the two Churchwardens, the two Overseers of the Poor, and eight other parishioners. (**Llancarfan Vestry minute book**, p. 10).

There follows in the Vestry minute book '*A Survey and Classification of the several Farms and Premises in the Parish of Lancarvan that the same may be Assessed to the parish Rates*'. (**Llancarfan Vestry minute book**, pp. 22-28).

Attendances at these Vestries were small. Only the farmers and substantial men of the parish who paid the poor rate took part; many of them were unable to sign their names. In Llantrisant for example they were summoned to meet in the church porch, but often adjourned to the greater comfort of one of the inns of the town—the Boot, the Butchers' Arms, the Angel, the Bear, or the Swan (**Llantrisant Vestry minute book**, pp. 255, 262, 264, 265). The meeting was announced by tolling the church bell, or by the 'Borough Bellman'. The Vicar gave notice of Vestry meetings in church on Sundays; written notice was sometimes pinned on the church door, but of course many people were unable to read at this time. (**Llantrisant Vestry minute book**, pp. 6, 27, 42, 46, 51).

In Llandaff parish, Vestry meetings were from time to time held '*within the Consistory of the Cathedral Church*'. But more congenial venues were found in that parish at the Red Lion or the White Lion; the duty of attendance was sweetened by an allowance of ale, payment for which regularly occurs in the Overseers' accounts (**Llandaff parish books**, P/53/40 p. 167; P/53/41 pp. 9, 14, 22). At Llandeilo Talybont there was a regular ration—

'*At A Parish Meeting held this 30th Day of April 1794 We the Church Wardens, Overseer of the poor and several other Inhabitants of the Parish of Landilotalybont Do Settle and Agree that there shall be a quart of ale to every Inhabitant that shall attend Vestries in each Vestry this present year. As Wittness our hands the Day and year above Written.*'
(**Llandeilo Talybont Vestry minute book**, p. 104).

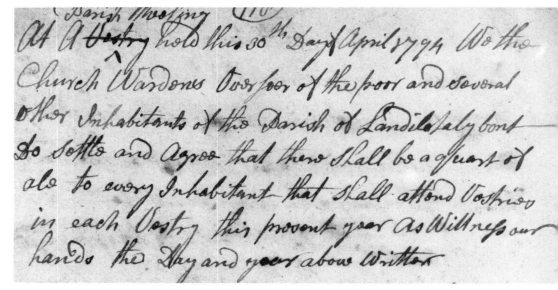

3   *Llandeilo Talybont*. Ale allowance at the Vestry, 1794.

At Llansannor in 1786, however, the parishioners had clearly seen the need to put a restraint upon parochial hospitality—

'*22th november 1786. It is agreed at a vestry held at the Dwelling house of Rees Adam in the Parish of Lansannor that the overseer of the Poor of the said Parish, when a vestry held, is to Pay for ale six pence for Each man, and whoever do Like to Drink more he is to pay for it himself.*'
(NLW, **Llansannor parish book**, p. 94).

Forty years later another parish sought to compel attendance by threats of financial penalties—

'*March 28th 1833. It is agreed between us the Parish[i]oners of Lancarvan in vestry asembled on account of having the Parish vestries better attended to, That one or more of the inhabitants of each hamlett within the said Parish are to attend the said vestries the first Thursday in every month throughout the year and should it be necessary to call vestry on any other particular buissness the same will be published in the parish church on the preceding Sunday and every hamlett that do neglect to attend at the time specified will be fined two shillings for non attendance.*'
(**Llancarfan Vestry minute book**, p. 55).

The Vestry decided the amount of the poor rate, the church rate and the highway rate which all occupiers of land and houses within the parish had to pay. The poor rate was usually fixed quarterly; the Vestry had to decide how property was to be valued, since ratepayers had to pay so many pence for each pound of the assessed value of their property.

'*Lantrissent Parish Workhouse. August the 5th 1785. At the Vestry held the said 5th day of August 1785*

Risolved that the poor Rates for the next Quarter Commencing this day be rated at One Shilling and Three pence in the pound.

Resolved that all the different houses in the Town of Lantrissent be rated Equally Alike at the fifth part of their real present value, And that the Mill called the Velyn Vawr Mill, And Also the Toll in Lantrissent Town be rated at the fourth part of their present Value.

Resolved that the rate of Sixpence in the pound be raised for the Church rate for the year 1785 …

Resolved that in addition … there be a List made out as soon as possible by the Overseer of the Town Hamlet, and that he insert therein an Impartial observation of All and every house wherein Dwelleth any poor who is not a parishioner at present or who may be likely to become a parishioner in paying the said Rates, in Order that the same may be excused as poor from paying the said rates' [and by so doing, qualify to receive poor relief in Llantrisant].
(**Llantrisant Vestry minute book**, p. 75).

In Merthyr Tydfil and in Aberdare the ironworks and associated coal mines constituted in the eighteenth and early nineteenth centuries by far the most valuable properties in those parishes, and were rated accordingly.

'At a Meeting of the Parishioners of Aberdare held for the purpose of Rating and Assessing the Furnaces belonging to the Aberdare Iron Co. since the Erection of their Forges at the same Rate and proportion that the Iron Furnaces in the Parish of Merthyr Tydvil—And that the Coal works belonging to Messrs. Crawshay & Co. are not paying Any Rates in the Parish of Aberdare being liable so to do—finding that the Quantity got each month is from 800 to a 1,000 Tons Averaging between 10,400 and 12,000 Tons a year at 6d. a Ton, Supposing the least number 10,400 raised annually would be £260 a year, the fourth of which is £65, We therefore order and direct a Rate to be made charging Messrs. Crawshay & Co. in our Parish Rate at £40 in each Quarterly Assessment. Dated 26th Day of April 1825. Witness THOMAS WILLIAMS Vestry Clerk J.B. BRUCE SAML. REES E.M. WILLIAMS RICHARD REES'
(**Aberdare Vestry minute book**, p. 65).

As the number of paupers and the burden of the poor rate increased, some parishes attempted to adopt a fairer system of property assessment for rating purposes. At a Merthyr Tydfil parish meeting on 22nd June 1832, for example, a new scheme of valuation was adopted. It was
'Resolved that in order equitably to arrange the Assessment of the Poors Rate of the Parish that the Lands of this Parish be rated at one third of their annual actual Value [and] that the Houses be rated at one Eighth of their Annual Actual Value and the Iron Works ... at £120 p[er] Furnace. Resolved that no dwelling Houses of a less Annual Value than Six pounds be rated to the Relief of the Poor, unless some business or Trade be therein carried on. [Signed as Chairman] J.J. GUEST.'
(**Merthyr Tydfil Vestry minute book**, p. 456).

But the Merthyr Tydfil Vestry was dominated by the ironmasters, who were determined to resist any increase in their contributions to poor relief. At a meeting in December a motion by Anthony Hill was carried, reducing the ironworks assessment once again from £120 to £60 per furnace.

The parish coffers were by now empty, however, (see below, p. 62), and the ironmasters were forced to make a substantial contribution to stave off insolvency and the breakdown of poor law administration. So, after the reduction of their assessments, and 'in consideration of which, Mr. Guest on behalf of the Dowlais Iron Co., and Messrs. R. and A. Hill on their own part, agree and will recommend to the Cyfarthfa and Penydarran Companies also to agree to pay among them the sum of £500, Towards enabling the parish Officers to diminish the existing debts of the parish to that amount'. (**Merthyr Tydfil Vestry minute book**, pp. 470, 471).

In addition to the proceeds of the poor rate, there was also in some parishes income from property bequeathed by benefactors to be held in trust for the benefit of the poor of the parish. Copied out into the Llandaff parish book for the period 1740-1749 there is for example a

'Clause in Mr. Illtid Nicholl's Will ... I give & devise two Cottages in Landaffe and an Acre and half of Freehold Lands situate near Cae Paine [owned by the Cathedral Chapter of Llandaff. Tithe apportionment, parish of Llandaff, no. 76] to ye

February tho 14th 1737/8

Delivered then by Anthony Maddocks of Boosney[?]
Gent: unto Evan Lewis Overseer of the poor of this parish
one bond from John Jenkins Gent: officer of Excise to
Thomas Rees late Overseer of the poor bearing date the
30th day of October 1728 for payment of Six pounds
with Interest. And also one other bond from John Hopkins
Gent: John Griffith Gent: and Walter Griffith Gent:
to the said Anthony Maddocks Gent: in trust for the poor
of Bettus bearing date the 10th day of May 1735 for
payment of twenty four pounds with Interest to that[?] said
two bonds are for securing the sum of Thirty pounds
Received by the said Anthony Maddocks from Anthony
Dowell Esqr to be laid out at Interest for the use of
the poor of Bettus.

Witnesses Present

Jno Bradford

Lewis Leyson

Tho Howell

William Leyson

4   *Bettws*. Money in trust for the benefit of the poor, 1737/38.

Vicar, Ch[urch]wardens & Overseers of ye poor of the Parish of Landaffe and their Successors upon trust that the s[ai]d Vicar, Churchwardens and Overseers and their Successors ... shall ... permitt ... two of the poorest widows Inhabitants of the s[ai]d Parish to ... receive the Rents ... of the s[ai]d two Cottages and the s[ai]d Acre & half of Lands for ever'.
(**Llandaff parish book**, P/53/38 p. 2).

Many philanthropic persons obviously considered that poor relief was inadequate, or indeed failed to provide at all for some deserving people. They therefore made provision in their wills, or during their lifetime, for gifts to the poor, as an expression of charity. The establishment and endowment of almshouses was a favourite form of benefaction. In 1670, for example, John Gibbs gave

'a house for the habitation of four poor widows, of the town of Neath, at the discretion of the churchwardens and overseers [of the poor] ... The house ... [subsequently enlarged] ... is situate in Water Street in Neath, and is capable of accommodating twelve objects of the charity. Behind the almshouse there was formerly a court or garden, upon part of which the parish, twenty years ago, erected a large kitchen, with two sleeping-rooms over it, and a stair-case leading into a house, which, at the same period they rebuilt for a workhouse, under a 21 years' lease ... [in 1836] the house is occupied by poor persons, put in by the parish, part of whom are in the receipt of parish relief.'
(**Report, Charity Commissioners 1837**, p. 399).

Sometimes the parish used bequests of money for this purpose. The 1837 Report records, regarding the *'Charities of Earl Talbot and Philip John'* in Pendoylan parish, that

'Earl Talbot, of Hensol, at a date unknown, gave the churchwardens and overseers of Pendoylan the sum of £50, the interest of which he directed should be yearly divided amongst the poor of the said parish; Philip John, by Will, dated in or about the year 1770, bequeathed £50 to the same use, and to be distributed in the like manner.

These sums, (having been previously otherwise invested) were, it is said, applied, by order of vestry, in the year 1817, together with £30 belonging to the parish, in erecting, upon parish land, six cottages, part of one of which is now occupied as a vestry-room, and the remainder are occupied rent-free, by paupers put in by the officers ... [As interest on these capital sums] £5 a year is regularly paid out of the rates and distributed by the vestry to poor persons not receiving parish relief, in sums varying, at their discretion, from 2s. to 10s. A regular account is kept of the application.'
(**Report, Charity Commissioners 1837**, p. 391).

Testators from time to time provided for the maintenance of paupers in parish almshouses by creating rent-charges upon their landed property; but with the effluxion of time their intentions might be frustrated. So it was reported by the Charity Commissioners in 1837 that

'Eleanor Matthews, of Aberaman ... by Will, dated the 15th day of March 1724, after reciting that she had built an almshouse ... for four poor persons for ever, in the village of Aberdare, charged all her lands ... in ... Glamorgan and ... Monmouth[shire] ... with the payment of the yearly sum of £5 towards the maintenance of the four poor

persons to be settled in the said almshouse ... [but by 1837] *This charity has long ceased to be applied for the purposes ... named by the testatrix. The almshouse, which consists of four distinct tenements, each tenement containing one room, has been for many years in the possession of the parish officers, who have been in the habit of placing in it four pauper women, amongst whom the rent-charge of £5 has been equally divided.*

The houses have been occasionally repaired, at the expense of the parish; but at the time of the inquiry [October 1836] they were in a dilapidated state. They were expected shortly to become vacant, in consequence of the parish of Aberdare, under the operation of the Poor Law Act [of 1834], forming part of the union of Merthyr, into which latter parish all the paupers of the union were to be removed. The property, which is liable to the payment of the annual sum of £5, consists of a farm, of about 50 acres, in the parish of Llanwonno, called Penrhugwrodoc [Penrhiw Cradoc], in the possession of J.B. Bruce, Esq., ... We have communicated with Crawshay Bailey, esq., the present possessor of the Aberaman estate, on the subject of this charity, and we apprehend that it will in future continue under his management and control.'
(**Report, Charity Commissioners 1837**, pp. 418, 419).

Distribution of relief in kind was frequently provided for by such private charitable trusts. For example, '*John Davies, of Neath, by Will, dated 25th September 1719, gave to the minister, churchwardens and overseers of Neath the sum of £26 to be laid out at interest, and the interest expended in providing 12 penny loaves every second Sunday, to be distributed to 12 poor persons of the said Town duly frequenting service at the church.*' (**Report, Charity Commissioners 1837**, pp. 397, 398). The Charity Commissioners also reported that '*Jane Thomas, by Will, dated 17th July 1761 ... gave to the poor of the parish of Llanmaes a bushel of wheat, of the Cowbridge measure, to be divided amongst them 10 days before Christmas*'. (**Report, Charity Commissioners 1837**, p. 390).

5   *Margam.* Dineley records John Brown's charity, 1684.

7

The bequest made by John Brown, who died in 1684, and who had been cook to the Mansel family at Margam, was noted by a contemporary traveller, Thomas Dineley, in his journal. Dineley visited Margam in the retinue of the Duke of Beaufort (*The Account of the Official Progress of His Grace Henry, Duke of Beaufort, through Wales in 1684*, p. 336). John Brown's charity, in a slightly modified form, is still distributed regularly in Margam, three hundred years later. A painted board listing the charitable benefactions made to the poor of a parish can often be found displayed in a parish church.

The terms of other similar bequests were modified by the poor law authorities as time went on.

'*Edward Morgan, by Will, dated the 22nd of February 1668*' had given '*out of his messuage and land situate at Torkington, in the county of Gloucester, twelve pence in bread weekly for ever, to be distributed to six poor people in twopenny loaves in the parish of Llanishen; in which distribution he directed that his poor kindred should be preferred, if there should be any there ...* ' But by the time of the 1837 Report, '*The annual produce, amounting to £2.12s is received by the churchwardens, and laid out in the purchase of bread, which is distributed by them, not weekly as directed by the testator, but on one day in the year, amongst such poor persons of the parish, in proportion to the size of their families, as are nominated at a meeting of the inhabitants in vestry.*'

(**Report, Charity Commissioners 1837**, p. 414).

Some such trusts failed in the course of time, as in the case of '*David Thomas's Charity*' in Eglwysilan parish in Caerphilly Hundred. The Commissioners' Report stated that

'*David Thomas, by Will, dated the 16th day of March 1709, devised an acre and a half of meadow or moor land to his son, William David, his heirs and assigns upon trust, on every 5th day of November, to buy and distribute so much flannel as the yearly rent of the premises* [i.e. the acre and a half] *would afford amongst such poor labourers, poor women, and other poor, as should not be registered as poor of the parish of Eglwysilan. And he nominated the said William David, his heirs and assigns, perpetual trustee and trustees and distributors of the said charity.*' Nevertheless '*in the return of 1786 ... it is added that the poor at that time received no benefit from it*' and by the time of the 1837 Charity Commissioners' Report, '*the charity ... appears to have been lost for many years past*'.

(**Report, Charity Commissioners 1837**, pp. 403, 404).

Land was conveyed to trustees to hold upon trust for a variety of charitable purposes. So

'*at a court baron, held for the manor of Talyfan, on the 21st January 1699, Evan Jenkins surrendered his copyhold lands to Howell Eustance and John Jenkins, and their customary heirs, as feofees, to hold the same to the use of the overseers and churchwardens of Ystrad Owen and Llanblethian, and their successors for ever, who were to let the lands from year to year, and to apply the rents ... in ... putting in order the tenor bell in the steeple of Llanblethian Church ... and ... in both parishes towards the repairation of the aforesaid parish churches ... and also to bind the poorest sort of children apprentices by consent of the parishioners; and likewise to relieve old labourers that should be unable to work.'*

(**Report, Charity Commissioners 1837**, p. 388).

The good intentions of Catherine Powell, of the parish of Llantrisant, to provide poor neighbours with milk, were eventually defeated by the passage of time. She,

'by Will, dated the 6th day of November 1739, charged one moiety of a messuage and lands called Trebannog ... which she devised to her nephew, Gervas Powell, in fee, with the expense of finding and maintaining thereon, for ever, one milch cow with summer and winter foddering ... for the use of seven poor people living next her mansion-house at Milton, to be nominated by her grandson and his heirs; and she further charged the same tenement with seven half-crowns, to be paid at Candlemas [2nd February], yearly for ever, to such seven persons as should have the benefit of the said cow.

It would appear, by the Parliamentary Returns of 1786, that, up to that period, the benefit of this charity was received according to the intentions of the testatrix.' But the 1837 Report concluded, *'For upwards of 40 years, however, it has been altogether discontinued'*.

(**Report, Charity Commissioners 1837**, p. 419.)

Trust moneys might also be lost, as in the case of *'Price's Charity'* in Swansea. The 1837 Commissioners reported that

'It appears from the Parliamentary Returns of 1786 that Captain John Price gave £200, the interest to the use of the poor.

This sum, instead of being invested, was deposited in the hands of the churchwardens, and was thenceforth handed down to successive churchwardens upon the balance of accounts, the interest being paid out of the church-rates, and distributed to the poor, until about 16 years ago, when Mr. Griffith Jenkins, the then acting churchwarden in whose hands the money then was, becoming insolvent, and the parish refusing to replace the money, the same was lost.'

(**Report, Charity Commissioners 1837**, p. 386).

CHAPTER TWO

The Impotent Poor

After the Civil War the central government made little attempt to interfere with the administration of the Poor Law by the parish vestries and the local magistrates. There was therefore a wide variety of practice in the parishes, even within a single county, reflecting from time to time very different attitudes towards the poor on the part of the vestrymen. As the number of paupers increased, however, towards the end of the eighteenth century, and the burden of the poor rate also, it is possible to detect a general hardening of attitudes, and an increased determination to reduce by any available means the financial liabilities of the parishes.

Some items in early accounts suggest that the Overseers of the Poor from time to time gave casual and unsystematic gifts to individuals by way of charity, as in the Llandaff account for 1710/11—

'Given out of Charity to a poor distressed Seaman .... 0—0—3[d.]
Given a poor woman & child by pass by the parish Consent .... 0—2—0[d.]'
(**Llandaff parish book**, P/53/37 f. 71).

But the Vestry soon realised that a check must be kept upon such disbursements—

'May ye 21th Anno D[omi]ni 1718 ... Ordered that noe officer be for ye future allowed any Sum or Sums of money given to Sailors, Soldiers or travellers w[i]thout ye p[ar]ticular Order & directions of one or more of ye Principal Inhabitants of this p[ar]ish in writing under his or their hand or hands.'
(**Llandaff parish book**, P/53/37 f. 140v).

If the pauper had a family, the parish Vestry looked first to them for his support. Fathers were made to pay for the maintenance of their sons and grandchildren, and sons, likewise, had in case of need to maintain their parents. In January 1785, for example, an action was brought at Quarter Sessions in Cardiff by the

'INHABITANTS OF LANTRISSANT AG[AIN]S[T] ROBERT JOHN.
On the Motion of Mr. William Humphreys, Attorney for the Inhabitants of Lantrissant & on due Service of Notice to Rober[t] John of this application to Court being moved, and Mr. Wm. Morgan, Attorney appearing for the said Robert John and defending for him, and on examination of the several Witnesses and Evidences produced in this Court, and on hearing what could be alledged by both partyes, IT IS ORDERED by this Court that Robert John the Father of Rees John and the

Grandfather of William aged 9 years, of Catherine aged 6 years, and of Rees aged 4 y[ea]rs, the Children of Rees John and Grandchildren of the said Robert John shall ... Weekly ... pay unto the Hands of the Churchwardens and Overseers of the Poor of the Parish of Lantriss[ant] ... the Sum of Three Shillings and Sixpence. It appearing in this Court that the said Robert John is of Sufficient Ability & that the said Rees John is very Poor—and unable & uncapable of Maintaining his said Children and the said Robert John do continue to pay the same till Legally discharged therefrom, AND it is further ordered that the Churchwardens and Overseers of the Poor of the said Parish of Lantrisant do pay the said Sum of Three Shillings and Sixpence to be received by them from the said Robert John weekly ... into the Hands of the said Rees John for the Maintenance and relief of his Children ... till further Order made concerning the same.

Signed *EDWARDS*
Clerk of Peace'

(**Llantrisant Vestry minute book**, p. 85).

Some Vestries however paid allowances to parishioners for keeping their relatives— '*Decr. 19th 1806. At a Vestry held this day* [in Merthyr Tydfil] ... *It is settle[d]* [that] ... *Ann Evans is to have five shillings a week till she swears her parish and if it is found that her parish is here she is to go to live to her sister who shall have five shillings a week for keeping her.*' (**Merthyr Tydfil Vestry minute book**, p. 104).

Such financial arrangements between parish and relative were sometimes executed by a formal Bond. Thus at the Quarter Sessions at Neath in July 1742 the inhabitants of the Higher Hamlet of Llangynwyd parish brought an action before the justices regarding '*Mary Richard otherwise John Widow of ye s[ai]d Higher Hamlet of Langonoyd being a Poor Woman and chargeable to ye s[ai]d Hamlet*'. As a result her son '*David Richard (being a reputed Person of Ability)*' executed a Bond by which he undertook to forfeit £100 to the Overseer of the Poor if he failed

'*at his ... own proper Costs & Charges ... well and sufficiently* [to] *relieve maintain and support the said Mary Richard his mother during her natural life with meat drink washing lodging Cloaths and all other necessaries fit and proper for the said Mary to the Clear Indemnification of the said Overseers of the poor ... and all other the Inhabitants of the Hamlett aforesaid*'. In return '*It was agreed in Order to Compromise the Same* [action] *that ye Inhabitants of ye Hamlet Should Pay or allow unto ye s[ai]d David Richard ye Sum of Eight Shillings Yearly towards ye House Rent or lodgeing of ye s[ai]d Mary Richard otherwise John dureing her natural life*'.

(**Llangynwyd parish records**, P/82/29/1).

The Settlement Act of 1732/33 (6 Geo. II c. 31) laid down that bastard children should be provided for by their fathers. The unfortunate mother was haled before a Justice of the Peace to make a sworn statement as to the father—

'*Glamorgan to wit The examination of Ann Rees of the Higher hamlet in the parish of Langonoyd in the said county singlewoman taken upon oath before me John Parry, Clerk, one of his Majesty's Justices of the peace in and for the said county this nineteenth day of December 1822 Who saith that on Monday the sixteenth day of*

December now last past at the dwelling house of Thomas William in the higher hamlet in the parish and county aforesaid She the said Ann Rees was Delivered of a female bastard child and that the said bastard child is likely to become chargeable to the said Higher hamlet ..., and that Thomas Rees of Surrowwy [Sirhowy] in the parish of Bedwellty in the county of Monmouth, Collier, did get her with child of the said bastard child

Taken and signed	*The mark of*
the day and year above written	*ANN REES*
before me	*X*

JOHN PARRY'

(**Llangynwyd parish records**, P/82/29/41).

A recalcitrant father might then be arrested by the parish constable in order to compel him to shoulder his responsibilities—

'*GLAMORGAN. To the Constables of the Paris[h] of Lancarvan to each and Every of them WHEREAS Jennett David of the Parish of Lancarvan in the said County, single woman, hath by her Voluntary examination taken in writing upon Oath before me John Bassett one of his Majesty's Justices of the Peace in and for the said County, this present Day declared herself to be with Child and that the said Child is likely to be born a Bastard and to be Chargeable to the Parish of Lancarvan ... and that David John, of the Parish of Port-cary Labrourer, is the Father of the said Child; AND WHEREAS Francis Morgan one of the Overseers of the Poor of the said Parish of Lancarvan aforesaid, in order to indemnify the said Parish in the Premises* [i.e. in the circumstances already stated] *hath applied to me to Issue out my Warrant for the apprehending of the said David John*

I do therefore order you to apprehend immediately the said David John, and to bring him before me or some other of his Majesty's Justices of the Peace for the said County to find Security to Indemnify the said Parish of Lancarvan, or else to find Sufficient surety for his apperance at the next General Quarter Sessions of the Peace to be holden for the said County, then and there to abide and perform such order ... as shall be made in pursuance of an Act passed in the Eighteenth year of the reign of her late majesty Queen Elizabeth [con]cerning bastards begotten and born out of Lawful Matrimony [18 Eliz. I c. 3] *—Given under my hand and Seal the 1st Day of May 1780.* [signed and sealed] *JOHN BASSET.'*

(**Llancarfan parish records**, P/36/2).

If, when the putative father was brought before them, the Justices decided that the case was proved, they made an affiliation order for payment to the parish authorities, who would otherwise have been liable for the maintenance of mother and child. These orders were numerous; they were usually made on a printed form, with spaces for insertion of dates, names and places, as in the case of the following:

'*ORDER OF FILIATION.*

County of Glamorgan. The Order of John Richardson Esq. and Edward Picton Clerk Esquires, two of his Majesty's Justices of the Peace, in and for the said County, (one whereof is of the Quorum) and both residing next to the limits of the parish-church within the Parish of Langonoyd in the said County, made the 11th day of February 1809 concerning a female bastard child lately born in the parish of Langonoyd aforesaid, of the body of Gwenllian Jenkin singlewoman:

ORDER OF FILIATION.

THE Order of *John Richardson Esq*. and *Edward Picton Clerk* Esquires, two of his Majesty's Justices of the Peace, in and for the said County, (one whereof is of the Quorum) and *both* residing *next to* — the limits of the parish-church within the Parish of *Langonoyd* — — — in the said County, made the *11th* day of *February* — 1809 concerning a *female* bastard child lately born in the parish of *Langonoyd* — — aforesaid, of the body of *Gwenllian Jenkin* — singlewoman:

WHEREAS it hath appeared unto us the said Justices, as well upon the complaint of the churchwardens and overseers of the poor of the said parish of *Langonoyd* as upon the oath of the said *Gwenllian Jenkin* — that she the said *Gwenllian Jenkin* — on the *sixth* day of *January* — now last past, was delivered of a *female* bastard child at *Tirbach* — in the parish of *Langonoyd* — in the said county, and that the said bastard child is now chargeable to the said parish of *Langonoyd* — and likely so to continue; and farther that *Thomas William* of the parish of *Juxta Neath* in the said county, *Labourer* — did beget the said bastard child on the body of her the said *Gwenllian Jenkin* — — — —

6   *Llangynwyd*. Extract from an Affiliation Order, 1809.

WHEREAS it hath appeared to us the said Justices, as well upon the complaint of the churchwardens and overseers of the poor of the said parish of Langonoyd as upon the oath of the said Gwenllian Jenkin that she the said Gwenllian Jenkin on the sixth day of January now last past was delivered of a female bastard child at Tirbach in the parish of Langonoyd ... and that the said bastard child is now chargeable to the said parish of Langonoyd and likely so to continue; and farther that Thomas William of the parish of Juxta Neath in the said county, Labourer did beget the said bastard child on the body of her the said Gwenllian Jenkin

We therefore, upon examination of the cause and circumstance of the premises ... do hereby adjudge him the said Thomas William to be the reputed father of the said bastard child.

And thereupon we do order, as well for the better relief of the said parish of Langonoyd as for the sustentation and relief of the said bastard child, that the said Thomas William shall and do forthwith, upon notice of this our order, pay or cause to be paid to the said

13

churchwardens and overseers of the poor of the said parish of Langonoyd ... the sum of Three Pounds and one shilling for and towards the lying-in of the said Gwenllian Jenkin and the maintenance of the said bastard child, to the time of making this our order.

And we do also hereby further order, that the said Thomas William shall likewise pay ... to the churchwardens and overseers of the poor of the said parish of Langonoyd for the time being ... the sum of Three Shillings weekly ... from this present time, for and towards the keeping, sustentation and maintenance of the said bastard child, for and during so long time as the said bastard child shall be chargeable to the said parish of Langonoyd. Given under our hands and seals the date and year first above written.

JOHN RICHARDSON
EDW. PICTON.'

(**Llangynwyd parish records**, P/82/29/39).

Such fathers of illegitimate children were frequently compelled to find sureties who would, with them, sign and seal 'Bastardy Bonds', guaranteeing the parish against any expenses resulting from the birth. Such for example was a Bond executed on 26th February 1779 by one *'Evan David, Yeoman, ... of the Parish of Langonnoyd'* and by his two sureties, in respect of the pregnancy of *'Jennet William of the Parish ... aforesaid ... Spinster'*, for which Evan David was responsible. The three men bound themselves, on pain of forfeiting their Bond of £40, to indemnify the Churchwardens, Overseers of the Poor and inhabitants of the parish against

'all manner of Expences, Damages, Costs and Charges whatsoever, which shall or may in any manner at any Time hereafter arise ... by Reason or means of the said Jennet William's being great with Child as aforesaid, or for or by reason or means of the Birth, Maintenance, Education and bringing up of such Child or Children, that the said Jennet William goeth with, and shall be delivered of; and of and from all Actions, Suits, Troubles, Charges, Damages and Demands whatsoever, touching and concerning the same'.

(**Llangynwyd parish records**, P/82/29/13).

Fees had to be paid by the parish officers at every stage of these proceedings. Thus the *'Account of John Howel of Kevenarda* [Cefnarda, a farmhouse about 6 miles NW. of Swansea; 2-inch Ordnance Survey manuscript map of 1813, Glamorgan sheet 179E] *one of the Overseers of the Poor of the Parish of Landilotalibont Begining may The 1st 1787 Ending Abril the 30th 1788'* recorded that he

[£ s. d.   ]

*'P[ai]d to Rees Morgan Constable for Going with Sara Vaugh
     to swear her Child* .... 0—1—0—0
Do. to the Magistrate for her Oath swearing her Child and parish .... 0—2—0—0
*Do. for a Warrrant ag[ain]st Rees Thos. on the Cause of the
     said Child* .... 0—1—0—0'

(**Llandeilo Talybont Overseers' account book** 1773-1810, pp. 138, 139)

Despite all their efforts, expense in some cases did of course fall upon the parishioners. So in Llancarfan *'At a vestry held May 30th 1821 ... it is agreed that John Giles Junr. is to have three Shillings p[e]r week for the keep of Ann David being pregnant duering the time of her Confinement and the parish to allow five Shillings for a Midwife'*. (**Llancarfan Vestry minute book**, p. 1).

The Vestry was apt to deal unsympathetically with such unfortunate young women after their confinements—

'At a vestery Heald this ye 18th day of martch 1788 At the parish Church of Landilotalybont By the Churchwardens and several others of the in inhabetance we do hearby setle and order John David our overseer of the poor To go to a magistrat to draw a warant against Elisabeth Evan That was Latly delivered of a feamal bastard Child and to Compel her forthwhith the said Elisabeth Evan To Bridwel as the law direct[s]. As witness our hands the day and year first Above writen.'

(**Llandeilo Talybont Vestry minute book**, p. 51).

Mothers might be compelled to hand over their illegitimate babies to the tender mercies of the Overseers of the Poor; thus at a Bettws parish Vestry meeting

'held at the Dwelling house of Thomas Young, Near Bettus Church, March the 27 1792, in occation of the Bastard Child of Mary Samuel of the Hamlet of Cwmdy in the parish of Langoyned all the persons who met in the said Vestry have agreed that John William our overseer shall pay no more money towards the maintenance of the said Bastard because the mother refused to deliver the said child to our said overseer in the presence of David Thomas'.

(**Bettws parish book**, p. 270).

By the nineteenth century the ratepayers of one Glamorgan parish at least felt very strongly that the support and maintenance of bastard children was an intolerable burden—

'Lantrissent Parish. The Vestry of the 20th January 1813 ...
We do hereby deem it necessary for the General good of the Parishioners at large, and to relieve the Poor Farmers of the said Parish, who labour under great difficulty to pay their poor Rates and other Taxes. And we are also grieved as Inhabitants of the said Parish seeing that we gather and Pay our money for and towards such improper Purposes as they are Paid, which can and may be proved by several and Respectable Land Owners and Substantial Farmers of the said Parish, aswell as the Officers of the Parish for the time being, there are Bastard children without any security given for them by their reputed Fathers to the Parish, Single women when pregnant after being Removed by Regular orders, they return again to the said Parish of Lantrissent to lie in, Married Men and Married Women cohabit with others unlawfully, Several young women make a trade of getting Bastard children, and live Idle, and we cannot suppose they live honestly, as they ought to do, And will certainly be the Ruin of Almost the whole of the Young Men of the Neighbourhood of the Town of Lantrissent. Some of these women have Nine Bastard children and others have two, three and four, and several of them have one Bastard child each, and we are determined to Prosecute those Characters as the Law directs.'

(**Llantrisant Vestry minute book**, p. 431).

In many cases, however, there was no relative or other responsible individual who could be made to pay, so that the burden fell upon the parish. The Vestry minutes consequently record large numbers of decisions and orders to help paupers who were incapacitated by age, sickness or other disability. These orders appear to be based upon no generally agreed system such as that agreed at Speenhamland by the Berkshire magistrates. Each Glamorgan parish exercised an apparently unfettered discretion as to the method and scale of relief. Sometimes they authorised payments to poor people of the parish in money, sometimes in food, clothes, blankets or fuel, and sometimes both in money and in kind.

Allowances of food were frequently given in measures of barley, which then formed the staple diet of poor people, either baked into bread or in some other form. So at Llantrisant on '*Friday the 26th Day of February 1773 ... it was resolved and agreed by the Majority of the Vestry then Assembled, That David John, Pauper, is to be relieved with one Peck of Barly for four Weeks*'. (**Llantrisant Vestry minute book**, p. 5). But as time went on, the number of paupers increased, so the Vestry decided on a bulk purchase of barley to relieve them— '*It is resolved and agreed ... to purchase so much barley as will support the poor people of the parish ... against freiday next and to Continue foreward weekly and Every week as witness our hands this 27th day of May 1801 ...*' (**Llantrisant Vestry minute book**, p. 261).

The Vestries also saw to the apprenticing of pauper children. A Vestry meeting in Penmark on 5 June 1800 agreed that parish pauper children were to be apprenticed until they were 18 years of age, and it was decided by lot who should be liable to take an apprentice. (**D/D F** vol. 79, p. 58).

In November 1786 the Llantrisant Vestry '*Ordered that all the Children of the age of Seven years now in the workhouse be apprenticed ...*' (**Llantrisant Vestry minute book**, p. 102). This was supposed to be a means of teaching poor children a trade, by which they could earn their living. But in practice the main concern of the poor law authority was to rid the parish of the burden of maintaining these unfortunate children, who were often handed over to local farmers to be employed as farm labourers and domestic servants. This mean procedure was effected with all the pomp of inflated legal phraseology, signing and sealing –

'*THIS INDENTURE, made the First Day of November in the Thirtieth Year of the Reign of our Sovereign Lord George the Third by the Grace of God, of Great-Britain, France and Ireland, King, Defender of the Faith, and so forth; and in the Year of our Lord One thousand seven Hundred and Ninety. WITNESSETH That Mr. John Evans and Mrs. Mary Williams (in the Room of her late Husband, Deceased), Church-wardens of the Parish of Lancarvan in the in the* [sic] *County of Glamorgan AND Mr. David Rees and Mr. Azariah Evans Overseers of the Poor of the said Parish, by and with the consent of his Majesty's Justices of the Peace for the said County whose Names are hereunto subscribed, have put and placed ... Margaret Jones Aged Twelve Years a poor Child of the said Parish, Apprentice to William David of Lanbethery in the said Parish and County, Farmer, with him to dwell and serve from the Date of these Presents* [i.e. this document], *until the said*

Apprentice shall accomplish her full Age of Eighteen Years (and from thenceforth to be entirely free from the said Master) according to the Statute in that Case made and provided [i.e. the Poor Law of 1601: 43 Eliz. I c. 2].

DURING all which Term the said Apprentice her said Master faithfully shall serve in all lawful Business, according to her Power, Wit and Ability; and honestly, orderly and obediently, in all things demean and behave her self towards her said Master and all his during the said Term.

AND the said William David ... doth Covenant ... with the said Church-Wardens and Overseers ... That the said William David the said Apprentice in [the] Craft Mystery and Occupation of a Dairy Maid after the best manner that he can or may teach instruct and inform or cause to be taught instructed and informed ... AND shall and will during all the Term aforesaid, ... provide ... unto the Said Apprentice, meet, competent, and sufficient Meat, Drink, and Apparel, Lodging, Washing and all other Things, necessary and fit for an Apprentice.

AND also shall and will so provide for the said Apprentice, that [s]he be not any way a Charge to the said Parish, or Parishioners of the same; but of and from all Charge shall and will save the said Parish and Parishioners harmless and indemnified during the said Term.

IN WITNESS whereof, the Parties abovesaid to these present Indentures, interchangeably have put their Hands and Seals, the Day and Year above-written.

Sealed and deliver'd	[signed and sealed by]
in the Presence of	*JOHN EVAN*
WILLM. EVAN	*MARY WILLIAMS Churchwardens*
	[the mark of] *DAVID X REES*
	[illegible] *AZARIAH EVANS Overseers*
	WILLIAM DAVID

We whose Names are subscribed, Justices of the Peace for the County aforesaid, (one of us being of the Quorum) do consent to the putting forth of the abovesaid Margret James [sic] Apprentice, according to the intent and Meaning of the above Indenture.

JNO. BASSETT
JOHN LLEWELLIN'

(**Llancarfan parish records**, P/36/6).

17

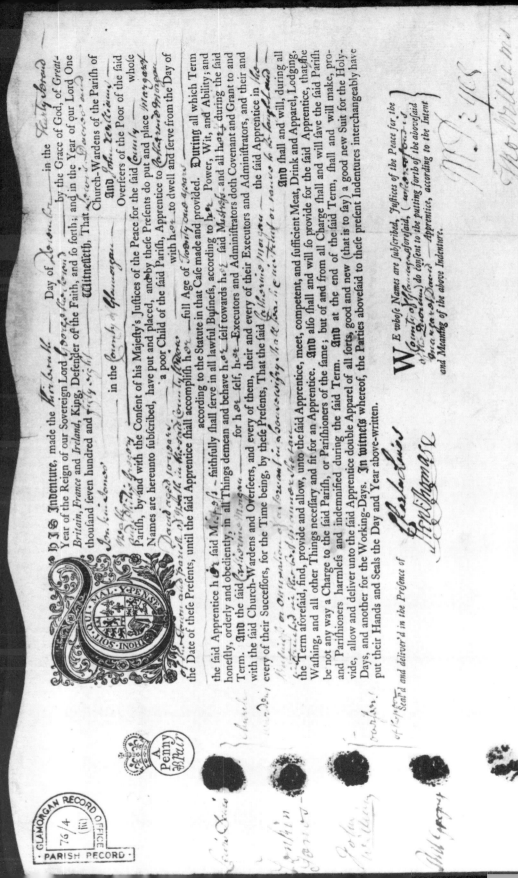

THIS Indenture, made the _Thirteenth_ Day of _November_ in the _Thirty Second_ Year of the Reign of our Sovereign Lord _George the Third_ by the Grace of God, of Great-Britain, France and Ireland, King, Defender of the Faith, and so forth; and in the Year of our Lord One thousand seven hundred and _Ninety eight_ **Witnesseth,** That _Henry Davies_ and _Jon. Evans_ Church-Wardens of the Parish of _Ystradowen_ and _John Williams_ Overseers of the Poor of the said _County_ whole Names are hereunto subscribed, by and with the Consent of his Majesty's Justices of the Peace for the said _County_ Parish, by and with the Consent of his Majesty's Justices of the Peace for the said _County_ Names are hereunto subscribed, have put and placed, and by these Presents do put and place _Margaret_ a poor Child of the said Parish, Apprentice to _Edward Spring_ with h_er_ to dwell and serve from the Day of the Date of these Presents, until the said Apprentice shall accomplish h_er_ full Age of _Twenty one years_ according to the Statute in that Case made and provided. **During** all which Term the said Apprentice h_er_ said M_istress_ faithfully shall serve in all lawful Business, according to h_er_ Power, Wit, and Ability; and honestly, orderly and obediently, in all Things demean and behave h_er_ self towards h_er_ said M_istress_ and all h_er_ during the said Term. **And** the said _Edward Spring_ for h_er_ self, h_er_ Executors and Administrators doth Covenant and Grant to and with the said Church-Wardens and Overseers, and every of them, their and every of their Executors and Administrators, and their and every of their Successors, for the Time being, by these Presents, That the said _Edward Spring_ the said Apprentice in _the_ _business of a housewifry & all kind of works belonging to husbandry_ shall and will, during all the Term aforesaid, find, provide and allow, unto the said Apprentice, meet, competent, and sufficient Meat, Drink and Apparel, Lodging, Washing, and all other Things necessary and fit for an Apprentice. **And** also shall and will so provide for the said Apprentice, that the said Parish be not any way a Charge to the said Parish, or Parishioners of the same; but of and from all Charge shall and will save the said Parish and Parishioners harmless and indemnified during the said Term. **And** at the end of the said Term, shall and will make, provide, allow and deliver unto the said Apprentice double Apparel of all forts, good and new (that is to say) a good new Suit for the Holy-Days, and another for the Working-Days. **In witness** whereof, the Parties abovesaid to these present Indentures interchangeably have put their Hands and Seals the Day and Year above-written.

Seal'd and deliver'd in the Presence of

WE whose Names are subscribed, Justices of the Peace for the _County of Glamorgan aforesaid_, do consent to the putting forth of the aforesaid _above named_ Apprentice, according to the Intent and Meaning of the above Indenture.

Chas. Lewis

Rd. Whitman.

Wm. Jones

Tho. Williams

A similar Indenture was drawn up for the Churchwardens and Overseers of Neath when they apprenticed the ten-year-old Margaret David to Catherine Morgan, a widow, of Neath. The term of apprenticeship was to extend until Margaret was twenty-one years of age, and she was to learn the occupation of a servant in housewifery. (**Neath parish records**, P/76/4).

Pauper children could be taken from their parents by the parish officers, on pain of forfeiting any claim to poor relief. At an Aberdare parish Vestry held on 5th November 1819, for example, it was

'*resolved that the apprentices which have been indentured, & whose parents have refused to let them go to their different Masters, be taken as soon as possible by the respective parish officers to such places. Resolved, that on no pretence whatever, relief of any description be given to the parents so refusing. Resolved, that the parish officers attend at 9 o'clock in the morning of Tuesday the 9th. Novr. inst. with lists of farmers or other persons in their respective Hamlets, fit to take apprentices—& also lists of children of nine years old and upwards, whose parents are now burthensome to the parish, that such children may be apprenticed on that day*'.

(**Aberdare Vestry minute book**, pp. 14, 15).

7 *Neath.* Apprenticeship Indenture of a pauper child, 1758.

The accounts of the Overseers of the Poor in Llysworney for 1776 itemise the purchase of cloth, buttons, and thread for making a coat, waistcoat, shirts and breeches, as well as the provision of stockings, shoes and a hat for Thomas Evan, a pauper child, and the drawing up of his Indenture of Apprenticeship. (**Llysworney Overseers' account book**, p. 12).

8 *Llysworney*. Money spent on clothes for a poor child, 1776/77.

It was a common practice during the early nineteenth century for Overseers of the Poor in English counties to pack off pauper children to sweated employment in textile factories; in Glamorgan there was at least one scheme for employing them in a 'Lace Manufactory'—

'July 22d 1814. At a Vestry held this day [in Merthyr Tydfil] *... in Order to set up a **Lace Manufactory** for the employment of the female Children of the Poor of this Parish; The following* [five] *Gentlemen ... are appointed as a Committee with the Church Wardens and Overseers of the Poor to agree with Mr. Montague to set up the said Manufactory ...*

10th Day of January 1815 ... Resolved that a certain number of Children not exceeding Forty be bound for Three Years from their commencing to James Montague to learn the Lace Trade upon the Terms agreed upon with him—he lodging them in his House and being allowed 5/- each p[er] Annum for their Washing—Resolved that those Parents who refuse to allow their Children to be put to the Lace Trade shall not recieve parochial Relief.

Ordered that the Parish officers frequently inspect the Children at their work & see that the Children are properly fed & cleaned & are well used.

Ordered that the Overseer find a sufficient Number of Beds to lodge the Children at Jas. Montague's House.'

(**Merthyr Tydfil Vestry minute book**, pp. 195, 198).

Ordered   That an agreement made by the Assistant Overseer with Phillip Jones Basket Maker, of paying him at the rate of 1 Guinea per Week for one Month, be conformed – and that the Overseer pay the Sum of £7„0„0 for 20 Bundles of Osiers. for the purpose of making Baskets. –

Ordered   That the Children, and others in the Workhouse be employed either in Basket Making & picking Oakum

9   *Cardiff, St. John and St. Mary.* Pauper children to make baskets or pick oakum, 1819.

The Parish sometimes took stern measures to deal with young paupers who were delinquent. On 10th November 1786 the Llantrisant Vestry

'Ordered that Thomas Cox Aged 18 years and David Cox Aged 14 are common Nuisances in the said Parish and that by their Consent the Overseers of the Poor of the said Parish do take them to Bristol and ship them at the most reasonable Terms to be made Mariners, with a Condition that if their Captain or Captains suffer any or either of them to escape, that he or they Give proper security to refund to the said Parish of Lantrissent the money rec[eiv]ed with the said Thomas and David Cox'.
(**Llantrisant Vestry minute book**, p.102).

A variety of means was used to look after sick and aged paupers in the parish. At a Llantrisant Vestry held on 26th February 1773, for example, 'it was resolved and agreed by the Majority of the Vestry then assembled ... That Ann Griffith is to take care of Martha Morg[an] during her illness at 1/6 p[er] Week'. (**Llantrisant Vestry minute book**, p. 7).

In other cases allowances in kind were given—

'December 24th 1784. At a [Llantrisant] Vestry held this Day, Resolved that 3½ yards of Flannen for one Shift, And 1 yard Flannen for one Apron be given Anne William (alias Evan) living in the Parish of Pendoylon, owing to her Old Age and Ill State of health being above Eighty Six years of age & Infirm.'
(**Llantrisant Vestry minute book**, p. 63).

Payments to a woman in need, during the last weeks of her life, and the cost of her burial, are recorded in the accounts of the Overseers of the Poor for Peterston-super-Ely for 1793/94 (**Peterston-super-Ely Overseers' account book**, p. 73).

Those mentally afflicted were looked after; in 1783 the Llantrisant Vestry resolved '... that Thos. Jenkins Daughter Idiot is to go to Mary Owen and she is to be allowed Weekly 2/6'. (**Llantrisant Vestry minute book**, p. 38).

On occasion the Vestry showed generosity in deciding to obtain for such unfortunate young paupers the best medical treatment available—

'Llantrissent Parish—At a Vestry held this 4th. day of January 1782 in the Church Porch ... and ... Adjourned ... to the House of John Evan, Victualler, and there to meet at 3 O'Clock in the afternoon. The Resolution of the Majority of this Vestry is that Thomas Jenkin of Rhubridwell [a farmhouse about ½ mile SE. of Llantrisant town; 2-inch Ordnance Survey manuscript map of 1811, Glamorgan sheet 177] is the Person nominated to take charge of Mary the Daughter of Jenkin David, an Insane Girl, and to deliver her into the custody of Bethlem Hospital in London to the Directors and Managers of the said Hospital for Cure; He being allowed the sum of £7 for their support and maintenance on the Road out of the Money lodged in the hands of Lewis Evan and John David for the support of the said Jenkin David's Wife, and family. The said Thomas Jenkin is to bring back with him for the safe delivery of the said Mary proper Receipts.'
(**Llantrisant Vestry minute book**, p. 31).

The Merthyr Tydfil Vestry in 1807 followed the current belief in the therapeutic value of bathing in sea water and even drinking it— 'June 23d. At a Vestry held this day ... It is settled ... Wm. Thomas is to give Wm. Daniel's wife two

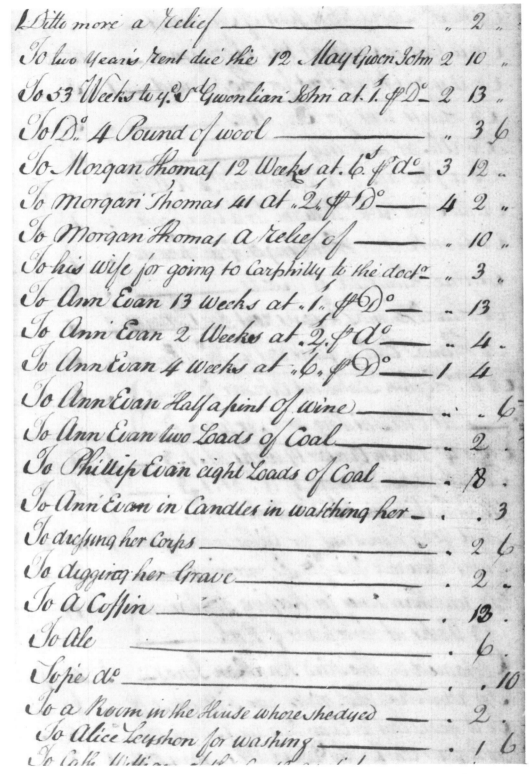

Description	£	s	d
Ditto more a Relief		„ 2	„
To two Years rent due the 12 May Gwen John	2	10	„
To 53 Weeks to y.e S.t Gwenlian John at 1. ⅌ D.o	2	13	„
To D.o 4 Pound of wool		„ 3	6
To Morgan Thomas 12 Weeks at 6. ⅌ d.o	3	12	„
To Morgan Thomas 41 at „ 2. ⅌ D.o	4	2	„
To Morgan Thomas a Relief of		„ 10	„
To his wife for going to Carphilly to the doct.o		„ 3	
To Ann Evan 13 Weeks at „ 1. ⅌ D.o		„ 13	
To Ann Evan 2 Weeks at „ 2. ⅌ d.o		„ 4	„
To Ann Evan 4 Weeks at „ 6. ⅌ D.o	1	4	
To Ann Evan Half a pint of Wine		„ „	6
To Ann Evan two Loads of Coal		„ 2	„
To Phillip Evan eight Loads of Coal		„ 8	„
To Ann Evan in Candles in watching her		„ „	3
To dressing her Corps		„ 2	6
To digging her Grave		„ 2	„
To a Coffin		„ 13	
To Ale		„ 6	„
To pe d.o		„ „	10
To a Room in the House where she dyed		„ 2	
To Alice Leyshon for washing		„ 1	6

10 *Peterston-super-Ely. Overseers' account of money spent on a poor woman, 1793/94.*

11   Thos. Lewis *alias* Tom Marlborough (Swansea castle in background), watercolour
by George Delamotte, *c*.1819

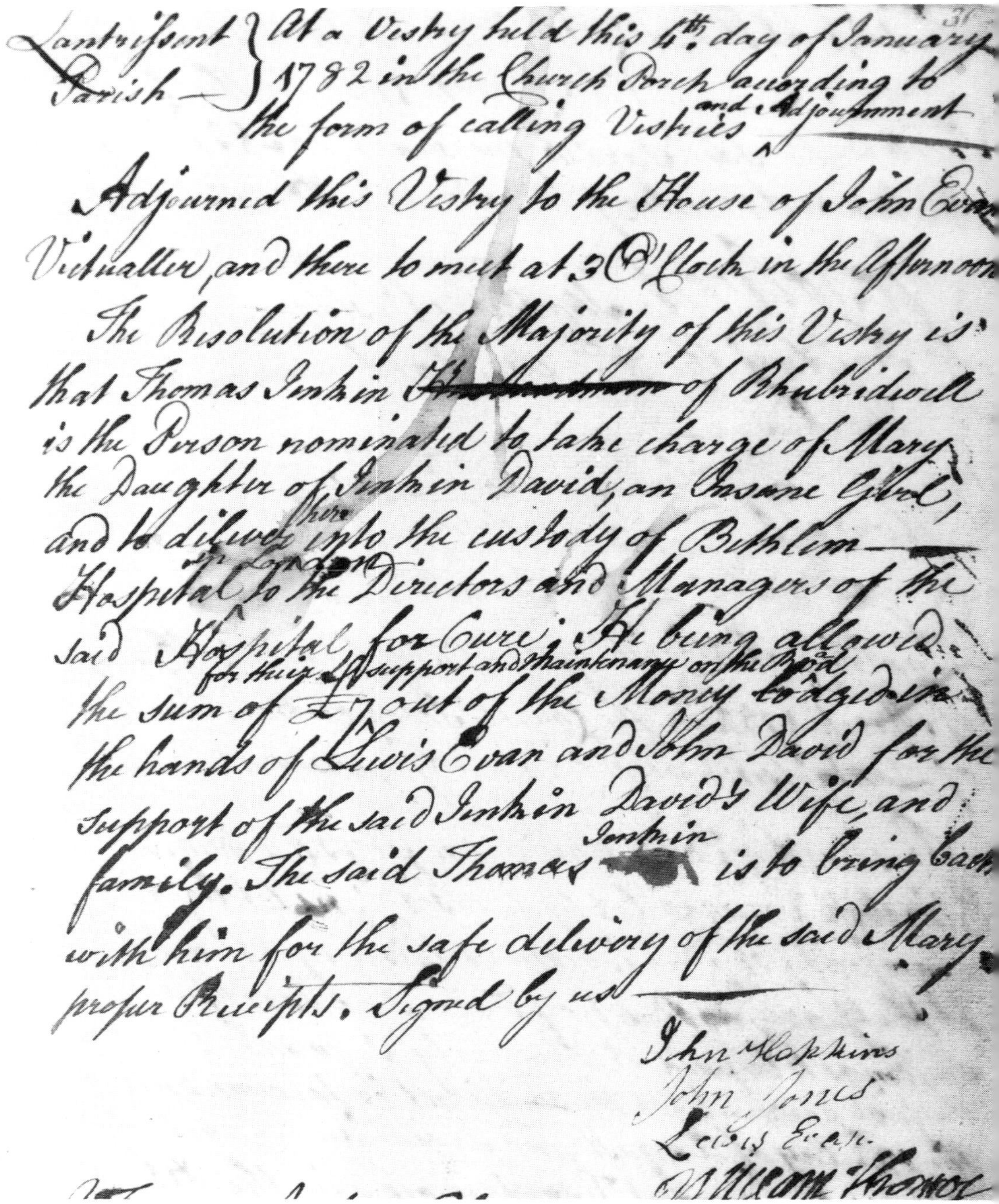

Lantrissant Parish } At a Vestry held this 4th day of January 1782 in the Church Porch according to the form of calling Vestries and Adjournment

Adjourned this Vestry to the House of John Evan Victualler, and there to meet at 3 O'Clock in the Afternoon

The Resolution of the Majority of this Vestry is that Thomas Jenkin ~~the Gentleman~~ of Rhubridioull is the Person nominated to take charge of Mary the Daughter of Jenkin David, an Insane Girl, and to deliver her into the custody of Bethlem Hospital in London to the Directors and Managers of the said Hospital, for Cure; He being allowed for their support and maintenance on the Road the sum of £7 out of the Money lodged in the hands of Lewis Evan and John David for the support of the said Jenkin David's Wife, and family. The said Thomas Jenkin is to bring back with him for the safe delivery of the said Mary proper Receipts. Signed by us

John Hopkins
John Jones
Lewis Evan
William Thomas

12 *Llantrisant*. An insane pauper child conveyed to Bethlem ['Bedlam'] Hospital, London, for treatment, 1782.

26

Guineas of relief to assist her to go to the Salt Water for her health...'
(**Merthyr Tydfil Vestry minute book**, p. 111).

The Aberdare Vestry likewise showed itself on occasion concerned to get the best medical treatment available for its paupers—'*At a Vestry held Sunday July the 18th 1819. It was resolved that the Overseer do as soon as Convenient take Richard Hopkins Son to Lanwyrtyd Wells to try and get a Cure for the Scurvy.*'
(**Aberdare Vestry minute book**, p. 13).

The Vestries appointed surgeons and apothecaries to attend the paupers of the parish when they were sick. On June 13th 1783, for example, the Llantrisant Vestry resolved

'*that Mr. Watkin Evans is is [sic] continued as Surgeon and Apothecary for our Parish in order to attend the Poor in all cases when afflicted, in the Surgery way or otherwise and supply them with Plaisters, Medicines, etc., and not only Poor Parishioners of our Parish but all Foreigners that either of the Overseers of our said Parish shall apply to him the said Watkin Evans for his opinion and Medicines, etc., at a Quarterly Salary of one Guinea commencing the 12th day of May last ...'*
(**Llantrisant Vestry minute book**, p. 39).

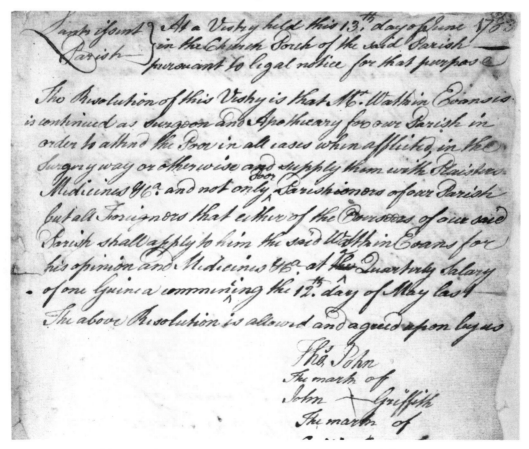

13 *Llantrisant*. Vestry appoints a surgeon-apothecary to attend the poor, 1783.

The responsibility of the Vestry for the paupers of the parish extended from the cradle to the grave. It paid carpenters to make coffins for them when they died—

'*Lantrisant May 13th 1773 Settled and agreed upon at a Vestry held this Day at the Dwelling House of Jno. Hugh Vict[ualle]r in the Borough of Lantris[an]t aforesaid by [and] between Abraham Rosser Carp[ente]r and the Parishioners that He the said Abraham Rosser engages to make Coffins at 7/6 each Coffin, large & small, for one whole Year from the date hereof in a decent and proper manner for interring the Poor of the said Parish, (provided God grants hi[m] leave)...*'
(**Llantrisant Vestry minute book**, p. 5).

The parish also paid part at least of their funeral expenses— '*August ye 2nd 1779. At a Vestry lawfully assembled this day at Aberavon it was agreed and ordered for the overseer of the poor is to pay one pound towards the burial of Janet David, late Dece[a]s[e]d.*' (**Aberavon Vestry minute book**, f. 14).

CHAPTER THREE

Able-bodied Paupers

Able-bodied paupers were to be set to work whenever possible. Female paupers were from time to time given the means to earn a livelihood at home. So in October 1767 the Llandaff parish meeting *'ordered that Elizabeth Jones is to have one shilling and six pence to buy her some hemp'* (**Llandaff parish book**, P/53/39 p. 249), in 1782 the parishioners of Llantrisant resolved *'that a Spinning Wheel ... be given to Cecil Evan'* (**Llantrisant Vestry minute book**, p. 34), and in 1814 the Vestry of Llandeilo Talybont agreed *'to relief Elizabeth Evan of five pounds of wool for making Shifts'*. (**Llandeilo Talybont Vestry minute book**, p. 207).

It was more difficult to find gainful occupation for male paupers; Llansannor parish showed enterprise and resource on one occasion at least—
'22th november 1786. It is ordered to the Pauper Thomas William Senior by order of a vestry held at the Dwelling house of Rees Adam that he is to have of Relife one shilling and six pence per week till the offisar of the Parish find him [a] Cupel of assis to Carry Cole upon in order to Clear the Parish from the occational relief of eighteen pence p[e]r Week.'

29

The Llansannor Overseer duly equipped Thomas William senior as a carrier: his accounts contain the following items—

> '*25th December. Paid for four assis* .... £*1-10-0*
> *Ditto. Paid for two baggs* *0- 5-0*
> *Ditto. Paid for two bagg sadels* *0- 4-2*
> *Ditto. Paid for shoeing the assis* *0- 2-0*
> *Ditto. Paid for two alters* .... *0- 0-6'*

(NLW, **Llansannor parish book**, pp. 94, 102).

There was no Prisoners' Aid Society in those rugged days; here again the parish came to the rescue. In April 1810 the Llantrisant Vestry '*ordered that Thomas Harry Miles is allowed to have the 10/- allowed him few days ago, towards defraying the Expences, coming out of Cardiff Goal, namely the fees to be paid Mr. Thomas Morgan the Goaler*[sic], *otherwise he could not come out to support himself or to endeavour so to do*'. (**Llantrisant Vestry minute book**, p. 379).

CHAPTER FOUR

Rogues, Vagabonds and Sturdy Beggars

The number of wandering beggars increased in the reign of Elizabeth I, so that in 1597 Parliament passed the Repression of Vagrancy Act (39 Eliz. I c. 4). By this Act any Justice of the Peace could order any *'Rogues, Vagabonds and Sturdy Beggars'* found begging outside their own parish to be punished. They were to be *'stripped naked from the middle upwards and openly whipped until his or her body be bloody, and then passed to his or her birthplace or last residence—and in case they know neither they are to be sent to the House of Correction for a year, unless someone gives them employment sooner'*.

14   A rogue and vagabond being flogged through the streets, 1577.

Accordingly, in eighteenth-century Glamorgan 'incorrigible rogues' who persisted in wandering and begging after conviction were sent to the House of Correction until the next Quarter Sessions. Here for example is a Justice's order committing a wandering beggar-woman—

'Glamorgan to witt—To the Constables of the Parish of Pyle and Kenfygg and to the keeper of the house of Correction att Cowbridge in ye said County—Greeting Whereas Margret John, otherwise Mary Lewis, widdow, a vagabond, was this day

found wandering and begging in ye Parish of Pyle and Kenfygg in the said County, not having obtained any legal settlement there, and was thereupon apprehended, and is now Brought before me Richard Jenkins, Esqr., one of the Justices of our Lord the King assigned to keep ye peace within ye said County, that she may be Punished and dealt withall, according to law, These are to Command you the said Constable to carry ye said Margret John to ye House of Correction att Cowbridge in ye said County and deliver her to the keeper thereof together with this warrant, and I do hereby require you ye said Keeper to receive the said Margret John into your Custody in ye said House of Correction, and her there safely to Keep until ye next General Quarter Sessions of the peace to be holden for the said County and have you her there, together with this precept. Given under my hand and seal this twelveth day of June in ye Eleventh year of the reign [of] our Lord George the third of Great Brittain, France, and Ireland King, Defender of the Faith and in ye year of our Lord 1700 and Seventy one -

[signed and sealed] RICH[AR]D JENKINS'

(**Q/S R** 1771C 70).

At Quarter Sessions the magistrates still enforced the barbarous provisions of the 1597 Vagrancy Act; on 6th April 1758, for example, they made the following order—

15 *Cowbridge.* A female vagrant to be whipped, 1758.

'Mary Jones otherwise Gordon otherwise Murray being brought Before This Court, And it Appearing that she is a Notorious Vagrant having endeavoured to Impose on the Inhabitants of ye Town of Swansea by saying she was marryed to one William Jones, a wine cooper of the same Town, which Appears to be false. It is Ordered that the said Mary Jones be stripped from the wast upwards and Publickly whipped upon Tuesday ye Eleventh day of April Instant between ye Hours of Ten and Twelve of the Clock in the forenoon of the same Day at ye s[ai]d Town of Cowbridge from ye East to the west Gate of ye s[ai]d Town.'

(**Q/S M** vol. 2, p. 178).

An Act of 1792 (32 Geo. III c. 45), however, brought this inhuman practice to an end; no female vagrant was henceforth to be whipped for any reason whatsoever. In the reign of William and Mary Parliament sought to lighten the burden of the poor rates in a less ferocious manner: it placed a public stigma upon all those in receipt of poor relief. An Act of 1697 (8 & 9 Wm. & Mary c. 30) provided that paupers were to wear upon their right sleeves a badge with '*a large Roman P* [for pauper] *and the first letter of the name of the parish ... cut thereon in red or blue cloth*'. During the next century Glamorgan justices from time to time tried to enforce this humiliating enactment. In 1738, for example, Quarter Sessions heard an appeal regarding relief for '*Robert Thomas, a poor Inhabitant in the Upper Hamlet of ye parish of Newcastle in ye s[ai]d County*' [of Glamorgan]. The Court ordered the Overseers of the Poor to pay Robert Thomas '*One Shilling and Six Pence a Week for and towards his maintenance, and It is further Ordered by This Court that the s[ai]d Robert Thomas Live and Reside within the s[ai]d Hamlet and that he also wears the Badge Ordered by Act of parliament ...*'

(**Q/S M** vol. 1, p. 363).

16   *Newcastle [Bridgend]. A pauper's badge to be worn, 1738.*

Parishioners attending a vestry meeting for Penmark on 31 January 1787 agreed that all who applied to the Overseer of the Poor for parish relief should wear a patch of blue or red cloth with the letters 'PP' (presumably for 'Pauper, Penmark') on their right shoulders. (**D/D F** vol. 79, p. 12).

The accounts of William Jones, Overseer of the Poor of the parish of Llandeilo Talybont for 1775-1776 include an item *'For Red cloth to put up the letters on ye shoulders of the poor and sewing up the same—1s. 11d'*. (**Llandeilo Talybont Overseers' account book**, p. 109). In 1740 the Overseer of the Poor in Penmark paid 6 pence for a quarter of a yard of blue material for making a pauper's badge. (**D/D F** vol. 79, p. 108).

17 *Llandeilo Talybont. Overseers' accounts include red cloth for paupers' badges, 1775.*

A later Poor Law Act of 1781/82, however, provided that paupers might be excused wearing the pauper badge *'upon proof of very decent and orderly behaviour'*. (**Act**, 22 Geo. III c. 83).

The House of Correction for Glamorgan paupers was in Cowbridge. It was maintained by a county rate, and the Keeper of the Gaol rendered his accounts to the Justices at Quarter Sessions. There is for example amongst the documents making up the Glamorgan Quarter Sessions Roll for Easter 1798 an *'Account of Expences on the house of Correction at Cowbridge from Jan[uar]y 10 to April 18th 1797'* submitted by Evan Deer, the Keeper as follows—

	[£ s. d.]		[£ s. d.]
'Prisoners Bill	4 6 9	'Attending the Q[uarte]r [Sessions]	
White Washing	10 –	at Cardiff	2 – –
Mops & Brooms	10 –	Conveying Margt. Preece from	
Sweeping Chimneys	7 6	the Quarter [Sessions]	6 –
Coal for the Prisoners	19 9	Thatchers Bill	13 6
Lime for White washing	5 –	Wm. Hary Bill for Reeds	1 7 4
Straw for the prisoners	1 5 –	Edwd. Rowlands Bill	6 9
Washing the prisoners Bed Cloase	10 –	Mr. Thomas Glaziers Bill	7 6
Cleaning the Nessesarys	7 6	P[ai]d Jenkin Jones for Cleaning	
Poor Tax for 1797	1 10 –	after the thatcher	4 6
Land and Window Tax	9 7	[Total] *16 12 8'*	
Church Tax	6 –	[one shilling out!]	

(**Q/S R** 1798B 91).

When a new county gaol was built at Swansea, the borough of Cowbridge bought the old House of Correction and converted it for use as the Town Hall, a purpose it still serves. The small cells in which prisoners were confined at night, and a larger room in which they could exercise during the day, can still be seen.

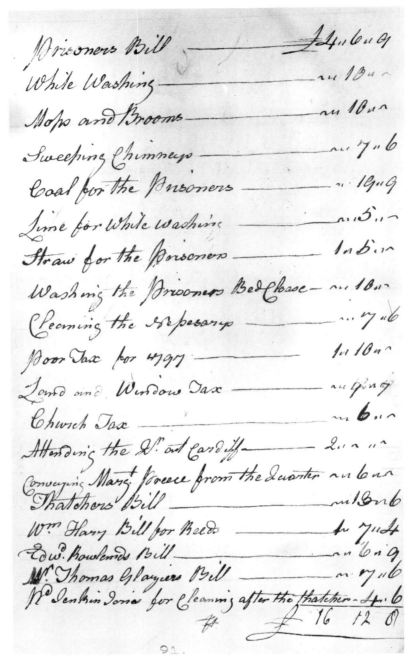

Prisoners Bill — £4..6..9
White Washing — ..10..
Mops and Brooms — ..10..
Sweeping Chimneys — ..7..6
Coal for the Prisoners — ..19..9
Lime for White washing — ..5..
Straw for the Prisoners — 1..5..
Washing the Prisoners Bed Clothe — ..10..
Cleaning the Repository — ..7..6
Poor Tax for 1797 — 1..10..
Land and Window Tax — ..
Church Tax — ..6..
Attending the D.r at Cardiff — 2..
Conveying Marg.t Preece from the Quarter — ..6..
Thatchers Bill — ..13..6
W.m Harry Bill for Reeds — ..7..4
Edw.d Rowlands Bill — ..6..9
M.r Thomas Glayiers Bill — ..7..6
M.r Jenkin Jones for Cleaning after the Thatcher — ..4..6
£ 16 12 0

91.

18 *Cowbridge.* Accounts of the Keeper of the county House of Correction, 1797.

CHAPTER FIVE

The Overseers of the Poor

Elizabeth I's great Poor Law of 1601 had laid down that the Overseers of the Poor were to be chosen from the farmers and substantial men of the parish who attended the Vestry meeting. They were appointed by the Justices of the Peace; with the Churchwardens they carried out the burdensome duties of collecting the poor rate and distributing it according to the decisions of the parish Vestry. The Llantrisant Vestry minute books, for example, show that in that parish there were five Overseers of the Poor, each responsible for one of the five hamlets into which the parish was divided—Town, Miskin, Gelliwion, Castellau and Trane (**Llantrisant Vestry minute book**, pp. 89, 90). They held office for one year and were unpaid; the Vestry Clerk, however, who kept the Vestry minute book, was a salaried official.

The duty of compiling lists of 'substantial householders' in each parish, from which appointments were made, fell upon the Overseers of the Poor for the time being—

'*Glamorganshire. Hundred of Newcastle.*
To the petty Constable of the Hamlet of Langony Higher in the parish of Langonoyd. By virtue of a precept from two His Majestys Justices of the peace in and for the said County of Glamorgan (One Whereof is of the Quorum) to me directed, you are hereby required immediate upon sight hereof to give notice to all and the Overseers of the poor within your Constablewick that they make out a List in Writting of a Competent number of Substantial Householders within their respective district, and deliver in the Same to the said Justices and others his Said Majestys Justices of the peace for the said County at Special Sessions to be holden at the Magistrates Office in Bridgend in the Said County Saturday the Twenty Ninth day of March Instant at the hour of Eleven O'Clock in the forenoon of the Same day, to the end that out of the Said list the Said Justices may appoint other Overseers of the poor for the year then next ensuing. And you are hereby also required to give notice to all Justices of the peace for the Said County, residing in your Constablewick of the time and place Appointed for holding the said Special Sessions. And be you then there to testify What you Shall have done in the premises. Herein fail you not. Given under my hand this 7th day of March in the year of Our Lord 1828.

WILLIAM LEWIS
Chief Constable'

(**Llangynwyd parish documents**, P/82/29/43).

The acount of Evan Mathew Oversee of
the Poor for the Parish of of Ystradowen
from May 1791 to May 1792
Disbousment as followeth

Paid Sara Evan 36 weeks at 2 p' week — — — —	3 · 12 —	
to 3 yards of Flanan for a shift to D° —	0 · 2 · 11	
D° for makeing and thred — — —	0 · 0 · 4	
D° for Taping her shoos — — —	0 · 1 · 9	
to bred and Butter the night shee died — —	0 · 0 · 8	
to candles and things — —	0 · 0 · 4½	
to Ann John for atening her in her sickness and dressing her Corps — —	0 · 3 · 0	4 · 19 · 7½
to Barbra Robort and Jenat Nichol for D°	0 · 2 · 0	
half a pound of shoop to wash her close	0 · 0 · 4	
for her coffing — —	0 · 10 · 0	
to the Parson — —	0 · 3 · 9	
to the clark — —	0 · 2 · 6	

19 *Ystradowen.* Overseer's account of money spent on a poor woman, 1791/92.

38

The Overseers had of course to keep accounts; the surviving Overseers' account books for Glamorgan parishes reduce the 'short and simple annals of the poor' to figures in a ledger. The sad little tale of the last days of Sara Evan of Ystradowen, for example, appears in the following itemized account—

'*The acount of Evan Mathew, Overseer of the Poor for the Parish of Ystradowen from May 1791 to May 1792*
Dispersment as followeth [£. s. d]
Paid Sara Evan 36 weeks at 2s. p[e]r Week ....*3 12 —*
To 3 yards of Flanan for a shift to D[itt]o *0 2 11*
[Ditt]o for makeing and thred....................................*0 0 4*
D[itt]o for Taping [i.e. mending]her shoos *0 1 9*
To bred and Butter the night shee died *0 0 8*
To candles and [?] rings *0 0 4½*
To Ann John for atening her in her sicknes and dressing her Corp's 0 3 0
To Barbra Robert and Jenat Nichol for D[itt]o *0 2 0*
half a pound of shoop to whash her Close..........................*0 0 4*
for her Coffing *0 10 0*
to the Parson..*0 3 9*
to the Clark ....*0 2 6'*

(**Ystradowen Overseers' account book**, p. 19).

The Overseers' accounts were examined by the Vestry or its agents; so in August 1781 the Llantrisant Vestry

'*RESOLVED That Two sufficient and able Persons be elected Annually out of each Hamlet for the examination of the Parish Accounts at each Parish Meeting which are quarterly and to rate according to the several necessities of the Poor as shall be adjudged best by them and the several Overseers for the time being; and that each of the several Persons so elected by the several Hamlets be allowed the sum of six Pence for their Quarterly Attendance, and to be paid or allowed out of the Poors rates ...*'
(**Llantrisant Vestry minute book**, p. 29).

Overseers were from time to time accused of misappropriation of Poor Law funds. Five Llantrisant Overseers were indicted on this count at the Michaelmas Quarter Sessions at Swansea in 1786 (**Llantrisant Vestry minute book**, p. 102); and on the 3rd of February 1802 it was

'*resolved and agreed by the Churchwarden and the overseers of the poor of the said parish [of Llantrisant], and the majority of the others parishioners assembled at the said meeting [of the parish Vestry] ... that Thos. Griffith overseer of the poor of Miskin Hamlet must aply to [a] Justice [of the Peace] for a warrant to aprehend Richard Bevan Late overseer of the s[ai]d Hamlet for money that he accounted in the parish account and not p[ai]d Which money are due to Mr. Vaughan, the attorney [for] Law Costs concerning Griffith Phillip, the whole Expences are to be Disbursed from the poor rates of the s[ai]d parish*'.
(**Llantrisant Vestry minute book**, p. 268).

It is not surprising that many parishioners were unwilling to undertake the

The Accompt of Mr. William Davies one of the
Overseers of the Poor of the parish of Llandaff
rendered to the parishoners of the said parish at
a Vestry or parish Meeting of the said parish held at
the Cathedral Church of Llandaff the 31.st Day of
May 1754

The Charge

Reced by Llandaff Rate	23	0	11¼
Canton Rate	23	11	0
Reced of my Predecessor in Office	7	10	9
Tot Charge	54	10	8¼

The Discharge

Paid Evan Jenkin and his Wife's weekly Allowance for 11 weeks at 2.^s p week	1	2	0
paid D.^o 41 weeks at 3.^s p week	6	3	0
paid Dorothy Applin 40 weeks at 1.^s	2	0	0
paid D.^o 4 weeks at 1.^s 6.^d	0	6	0
Elizabeth Morgan	2	12	0
Mary Penry	2	12	0
Edward Toby at 1.^s 6.^d p week	3	18	0
George Harry's son 15 weeks at 1.^s 6.^d p week	1	2	6

20 *Llandaff.* Extract from Overseer's accounts, 1754.

duties of Overseers of the Poor, or to pay a substitute, and that from time to time the parish Vestry had to resort to stern measures to compel them to do so—

'Lantrisant Parish. At a Vestry held this 7th day of June 1809, at the Bear Inn in the Town of Lantrisant aforesaid ... It is resolved and agreed by us ... Church-Warden, Overseers of the Poor and the other Inhabitants assembled at the said Vestry Ordered that James Jacob our Clerk is desired to write a Letter to Edward Evan of Trideigan [a farm about 1½ miles NE. of Llantrisant town; Ordnance Survey manuscript map of Glamorgan of 1811, sheet no. 177] *and Request* [him] *immediately without loss of time,* [to] *Submit to the orders of His Majesty's Justices of the Peace, appointing him an Overseer of the poor, and assume to himself the said office, for the Hamlets of Town and Gelliwion, or pay Wm. John of the George in the said Town of Lantrisant the sum of Five Pounds and Five Shillings for serving the said office of overseer for the said Hamlets, and to desire him to give a direct answer, or else on non compliance to be Indicted at the Next General Quarter Sessions, for not obeying the Justices's order ...'*

(**Llantrisant Vestry minute book**, p. 358).

When paupers died, their goods and chattels became the property of the parish; it became usual for the Vestry to instruct their officers to make inventories of paupers' effects, so that the parish should not be cheated on their demise. So it was that in June 1783 the Llantrisant Vestry

'resolved that John Foster, Overseer of the Poor of Gellŷwŷon Hamlet in the said Parish, is to go to the Parish of Bidwellty and there to inspect thoroughly and to give a just account of all the Household Furniture and other Effects belonging to one Lewis John, formerly living at Gellywyon vawr in our said Parish, and the said John Foster is to be allowed for his trouble five shillings.'

(**Llantrisant Vestry minute book**, p. 40).

Some of these pitiful inventories have been formally recorded in the Vestry minute books, such as the

'Account of Household goods the Property of [the] Parish of Lantrissent in the dwelling H[ouse] of Sarah Thomas, Widow, taken this 16 day [of] March 1810 by James Jacob Churchw[arden] and Edward William overseer of Miskin [Hamlet] and Wm. John of the George then Prese[nt]. 1 Chaff Bed—1 Rug—two Blank[ets]—1 Chaff Bolster—1 Bedstead—two stools—1 bench—1 Earthenware Dish and Small Jug— [?1Cup] and Saucer and 1 Teapot, 1 Teakettle, 1 Sp[inning] Wheel—1 large Earthenware dish—1 Frying [Pan]—1 Small Tongs and an Wooden Shovel.'

(**Llantrisant Vestry minute book**, p. 1).

The meagre effects of deceased paupers were sold by public auction –

'Butcher's Arms. Lantrissent Parish.

At a Vestry held this 20th day of January 1803 by Publick Notice given for that purpose it is resolved by the Churchwardens & Overseers of the Poor & the other Inhabitants assembled to Order the Hous[e]hold Goods of the late John Jones to be Deposited & Lodged in a Room in his late Dwelling House till Friday next & at that time to be disposed of to the highest Bidder.

Also Order'd the Goods sold & Deliver'd to be returned immediately from Thomas

James & Mary Howells & others & lodged as above. The sale of the said Goods to be on Friday 28th Inst. at 12 o'Clock. Also the wearing apparel & cloth[ing] of the said John Jones to be deliver'd to his nephew Evan Jones ... immediately by the Town Overseer Wm. Glascott.'
(**Llantrisant Vestry minute book**, p. 278).

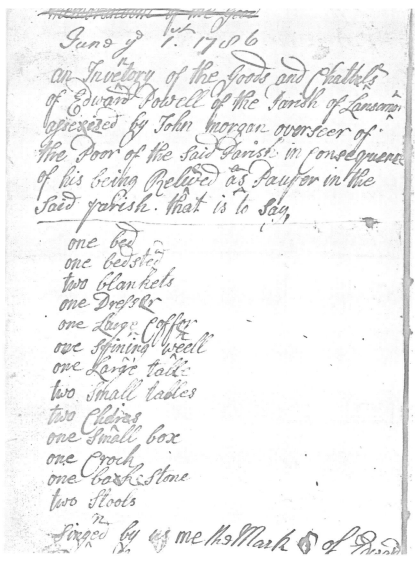

21 *Llansannor.* Inventory of a pauper's possessions, 1786.

CHAPTER SIX

The Parish Workhouse

Under the Old Poor Law, most poor relief was 'outdoor relief'—that is to say, payments in money or in kind were made to paupers who continued to live in their own homes. It was of course the Poor Law Amendment Act of 1834 (4 & 5 Wm. IV c. 76) which ushered in the era of the dreaded Union Workhouse. But long before that, poor-houses had been set up in individual parishes as refuges for those who could not support themselves, such as orphans, old and infirm people, bedridden invalids and lunatics. The rising costs of poor relief had spurred Parliament to action in this direction. Knatchbull's Act of 1722/23 (9 Geo. I c. 7) had enacted that in individual parishes the Churchwardens and Overseers of the Poor, with the consent of the majority of the inhabitants, might purchase buildings to be used as a workhouse, where able-bodied paupers might be set on work; anyone refusing to enter it was to lose all title to relief. It was hoped thereby to reduce the numbers of paupers receiving relief, and so the burden on the poor rate.

Accordingly on 23rd September 1740 the Llandaff Vestry *'ordered that every person who receives relief from the parish shall be lodged in the alms house till the same is full, upon pain of having their allowances withdrawn and for their Better accommodation the overseers are to putt the said house in good repair and cause a Bog house* [latrine] *to be built there in the most convenient place'.* (**Llandaff parish book**, P/53/38 p. 9).

Parish workhouses, however, proved quite inadequate to accommodate the rising number of paupers, so in 1782 Gilbert's Act provided that *'no person shall be sent to such poor house or houses, except such as are become indigent by old age, sickness or infirmities, and are unable to acquire a maintenance by their labour; and except such orphan children as shall be sent thither by order of the guardian, or guardians of the poor, with the approbation of the visitor; and except such children as shall necessarily go with their mothers thither for sustenance'.* Able-bodied persons who could not get work were to be found employment by the poor law authorities, and, if necessary, have their wages supplemented from the poor rate (**Act**, 22 Geo. III c. 83 ss. 29, 32).

In 1783 Llantrisant set up a parish workhouse, but the provisions of Gilbert's Act were not strictly adhered to. On 5th December *'a Vestry or public Meeting'* was held in the parish church *'to consult in regard of establishing a Workhouse etc. for the Poor of Lantrissent'.* The resolutions there made were declared to have been agreed to by *'the major part of the Parish of Lantrissent who have at this Vestry assembled'*. The two Churchwardens, four Overseers of the Poor, and eleven other parishioners did in fact sign the minutes or make their marks. It was *'1st RESOLVED That a Workhouse be established in or near the Town of Lantrissent for relief of the Poor of the said Parish of Lantrissent and setting the said Poor to work and so forth. 2nd. RESOLVED That John Popkins of Talygarn Esqr. and Mr. Evan Jones be appointed ... and vested with full Power ... in behalf of ... the said Parish to ... purchase, or rent, build or erect one or more House or Houses for the purpose aforesaid'*.

Trustees were appointed, including the Vicar, Churchwardens and Overseers of the Poor, the Portreeve and Town Clerk, and thirteen others, who were landowners or farmers. They were to superintend the workhouse and inspect the accounts, which were to be settled quarterly at a *'public Vestry'*. (**Llantrisant Vestry minute book**, pp. 42-45).

On May 5th of the next year the Vestry appointed *'Mary Frances and Rachel Frances, her sister'*, to be superintendents of the workhouse at an annual salary of £10 a year. Workhouse objectives and rules were agreed upon and recorded in the Vestry minutes. The poor of the parish were to be *'humanely and properly treated'*. The workhouse mistresses were to look after them, *'setting the same to work and to see them fed and kept in Order'*. The able poor were to *'assist the Governess in keeping the Houses Clean makeing the Beds Brewing bakeing & Boiling together with every other matter necessary to be done towards the health and Cleanliness of the said Poor & the said Houses,'* ... *'Only Married people'* were to *'be Lodged in the same room and a Partition to be made between Bed & Bed before they go to the poorhouse'*. The paupers' *'weekly Diet'* was to be *'settled and approved'* by the Vicar. Provision was made for medical attention for them. *'Watkin Evan, Surgeon'* was to *'Constantly and Daily attend the poor in the workhouse And Administer the usual necessarys wanting on those Occasions when sick'*; his fee was fixed at eight guineas a year, payable quarterly.

An attempt was made to provide against maladministration and misappropriation. The two workhouse governesses, *'if disapproved of'*, could *'be turned off at any Quarter's End by a Publick Vestry'*. It was further *'Resolved that no Person whatsoever make a Job* [i.e. dishonest profit] *of this Workhouse by buying any kind of necessarys for the use of the said house, of any relation; and that no overseer sell or buy of any Brother Officer any Commodity for the said poor'*. One of the Overseers of the Poor was appointed to purchase supplies for the workhouse. He was to keep accounts; the other Overseers were to *'attend as a Check on him and pay for the same or see him pay the money and that the same be entered by him in a Book kept for that purpose and signed by the other Overseers as an Approbation of the fairness of his Conduct'*. (**Llantrisant Vestry minute book**, pp. 54, 55).

These laudable resolutions notwithstanding, the Llantrisant Vestry sometimes found itself the victim of sharp practice. In May 1786 the parishioners resolved that
'WHEREAS it appears to us on Inspection that the Corn bought for the Workhouse by Joseph John is not fit to be kept for the use of the Poor, he is at Liberty to take to all the said Corn and to have a reasonable time to remove the same out of the Workhouse, And

At a Vestry held this 28th Day of September in the year 1790 within the parish Church of Landilotalybont, we the Church wardens overseers of the poor and several others of the Inhabitants of the said parish Do hereby mutually agree to rent a House of garden and Croft Morgan Morgan Called Penkefenarda Situate lying and being within parcel Piry Brenin within the sd parish at the yearly Rent or sum of Two pounds Two shillings, to be entered upon the 29th of this Instant, the repairs of the said House to be upon the sd morgan Morgan and likewise we Do hereby Covenant and agree to and with David Mathew for the maintenance washing fireing and all other Neessaries for the paupers of the said parish that Shall Come under his Care within the afore said House, at the rate of two shillings pr week to pauper wearing apparel and Burials Excepted, and Likewise we do hereby Disanull all other former agreements Concerning our said paupers and likewise that no relief shall be given to any person or persons that shall refuse to Come to the sd House Exceeding Six pence, and we Do hereby order oure overseers to provide as much bed Cloathes as shall be Sufficient

22 *Llandeilo Talybont*. Vestry arranges rented poor-house accommodation, 1790.

*we do hereby unanimously Rescind and make Void the Order of Vestry ... Ordering the
Overseers of this Parish to pay unto the said Joseph John £124 19s. ...'*
(**Llantrisant Vestry minute book**, p. 91).

This parish kept cows to supply milk for the workhouse inmates. In
November 1785 the Vestry decided

*'that Whereas it appears unto us that one of the parish Cows belonging to the
Lantrissant Workhouse is become Short of Milk, And that it is for the Advantage of
this parish to have the said Cow sold or exchanged for a more Milchy Cow, We do
therefore desire that Mr. Thomas David of Lwynypenne* [Llwyn-y-penau, a farmhouse near Groes-faen; 2-inch Ordnance Survey manuscript map of 1811, sheet
177] *(our present Churchwarden) do sell or dispose of the above Cow & purchase
Another in her room the most proper for the use of this parish according to his Judgment'.*
(**Llantrisant Vestry minute book**, p. 78).

23   *Llantrisant.* Milk for the parish workhouse, 1785.

The policy of this Vestry relating to admissions to the parish workhouse
changed from time to time, in accordance with the number of applicants and
the burden on the poor rate. In May 1786 it was resolved, in accordance with
Gilbert's Act, that *'WHEREAS the Workhouse was made in Order to Maintain and
provide for the Aged & Infirm and it appearing to this Vestry that Thomas Nicholas
and his Wife and Ann Stradling are able to work & maintain themselves; the Overseers
are hereby Ordered to discharge them out of the Workhouse'.*
(**Llantrisant Vestry minute book**, p. 91).

In November of the same year the Vestry dealt with a number of problems relating to the workhouse. Inmates were going out to work to supplement their allowance. To put a stop to this practice, the Vestry

'Ordered that no poor be suffered to go out to work to earn Money on their own accounts but if they'r able to work that they be put in the first Place to do all the necessary Buissnesses in the House and after that if they have spare time that the Overseers do put them to do other work, and to allow them a small matter out of their wages that they Earn if they earn any by way of encouragement and if they go out to work on their own Account without leave that the Governess do not permit them to Return back into the House and that if any of the Poor in the Workhouse behave in a Disrespectful manner to the Governess she is hereby impowered to Abridge them of their usual allowance of Victuals'.

Outdoor relief was to be strictly limited; it was

'Ordered that no Relief be given by any Parish Officer of this Parish to any Poor Person applying for the same not being resident in the workhouse without the approbation of the Revd. Robert Rickards Cl[er]k and Edmund Traherne Esqr. the only acting Justices for the Hundred of Miskin unless at a Publick Vestry held for this Parish'.
(**Llantrisant Vestry minute book**, p. 102).

The mounting expenditure on poor relief during the following years appears to have impelled the Llantrisant Vestry to panic measures. On the 4th of February 1801 the Churchwardens, Overseers of the Poor and

'the Majority of the other parishioners asembled at the s[ai]d meeting' agreed 'to Command all the paupers of the said parish immediately to the workhouse. It is also agreed ... with Mr. Thos. Rymbron to Look over the s[ai]d paupers and provide for them for ten pounds wages from the date hereof to the 12th day of may next, and the s[ai]d Thos. Rymbron are to rec[ei]ve so much sum of moneys as will be Necessary for the Maintenance of the s[ai]d paupers weekly from the present Overseers'.
(**Llantrisant Vestry minute book**, p. 256).

Llandeilo Talybont was another parish which set up a poor-house at about this time. In 1790 the Vestry rented 'a House garden and Croft ... Called "Penkefen-arda"' [see above, p. 14] at Tir-y-Brenin for £2 2s. od. a year; the landlord was to be responsible for repairs. The arrangements were as follows—

'We the Church wardens, overseers of the poor and several others of the Inhabitants of the said parish ... Do hereby Covenant and agree to and with David Mathew for the maintenance, washing, fireing and all other Nec[e]ssaries for the paupers of the said parish that shall Come under his Care within the aforesaid House at the rate of two shillings p[e]r week p[e]r pauper, wearing aparel and Burials Excepted ... and likewise that no relief shall be given to any person or persons that shall refuse to Come to the s[ai]d House exceeding Six pence and we Do Hereby order oure overseers to provide as much bed Clo[t]hes as shall be sufficient for three bedes, and also we Do hereby likewise order our afores[ai]d Overseers to purchase the worth or value of one pound one shilling of bed Clothes and other Necessaries and to Deliver the same unto John Bevan pauper of our said parish ...'
(**Llandeilo Talybont Vestry minute book**, p. 78).

CHAPTER SEVEN

The Laws of Settlement and Removal

Responsibility for the poor had been devolved by Tudor Parliaments upon the occupiers of property in the parish; as the burden of the poor rate increased in succeeding centuries, so Parliament reflected the determination of the rate-payers not to be burdened with paupers coming in from outside. The Settlement Act of 1662 (14 Car. II c. 12) provided that any workman who came into a strange parish was liable to be arrested by the constable and brought before a Justice of the Peace to give an account of himself on oath. This intolerable interference with the freedom of Britons to travel about to seek work was modified by a subsequent Act of 1794/95 (35 Geo. III c. 101) which provided that such poor persons were not to be subjected to this treatment until they were actually chargeable, e.g. made application for poor relief, or were found begging.

The purpose of these proceedings was to find out where the pauper had his legal 'settlement'—that is, which parish was legally bound to maintain him if he became ill, disabled or unemployed. Most workers had a settlement in the parish in which they were born, and their wives could obtain it by marriage. But a man could also get a settlement by owning and living on freehold land in the parish, or by serving an apprenticeship there, or serving as a hired servant for a year, or by paying the local rates, or by serving in one of the parish offices, such as parish constable, surveyor of the highways, or overseer of the poor [Settlement Act 1691 (3 Wm. & Mary c. 11), a consolidating statute].

Depositions of arrested persons, made before a Justice of the Peace, can sometimes be found among the records of Quarter Sessions, and provide moving evidence of the hardships suffered by unfortunate poor people, and the callous indifference of society at that time. The following, for example, is the story of a seaman in the Royal Navy, blinded on active service, and then paid off and reduced to begging, with his wife, for their bread—

'Glamorgan to wit. The Examination of Alexander Culbert a Rogue & Vagabond taken upon Oath before me Gabriel Powell one of his Majesty's Justices of the Peace in & for the s[ai]d County, on Thursday the 8th day of October in the year of our Lord 1772.

The said Examinant saith that he was born somewhere near Cork in the Kingdom of Ireland, that his Father was an American and he was carryed to Philadelphia when he was young, & that he served an Apprenticeship on Board a Ship belonging to one Mr.

Joseph Pemberton a merchant in Philadelphia, that about 13 or 14 years ago he was prest at Halifax in North America on Board the Fogeaux, Capt[ai]n Sprey, that about 12 years ago he was turn'd over to the Terrible, Captn. Collins, that about 13 years ago he was turn'd over at Woolwich to the new Thunder, Captn. Proby, & sail'd to the Mediterranean, that in reefing the Main Topsail, one of the reef Points struck him in the left Eye, w[hi]ch he lost, And the Anguish & Pain of that blinded his right Eye, he was then sent home to Portsmouth in the Wager a twenty gun ship, but who was the Captn. of her, he has forgot, And that the Fleet in the Mediterranean was then commanded by Admiral Saunders; that he was paid off at Portsmouth & turn'd adrift, that he then sent to his wife who then lived at Honiton in Devonshire, & whose maiden name was Deborah Bridle And marryed to him ab[ou]t 15 years ago in Stonehouse Church between Plymouth and [the] Dock, that since his discharge at Portsmouth he has travell'd about, that in Towns he is lead by a Dog & begs and his wife sells Laces, Garters & other trifling things without any Licence, and he has continued begging until he was taken up this day in the Town of Swansea as he was begging in the Street.

Sworn at Swansea in the   X
s[ai]d County before me   *The mark of*
GAB[RIEL] POWELL   *ALEXANDER CULBERT'*
(**Q/S R** 1773A 24).

Another such examination reveals the life history of John Price, found begging in Margam in 1770 (**Q/S R** 1770A 93).

After examining the pauper on oath, the Justice of the Peace might then sign and seal a Removal Order, ordering that he, and his wife and children if he had any, should be sent back to the parish which the Justice considered on the evidence to be legally responsible to maintain them. For example, on 25th June 1759 two Cardiff Justices of the Peace examined on oath one David Rosser, and then made the following order—

'*Cardiff Town—To wit. To The Constable, Headborough, Tythingman, and other Officers of the Peace of the parish of St. John the Baptist, in the Town of Cardiff to receive and convey, And to the Church-Wardens, Chapel-Wardens, or Overseer of the Poor of the Parish, ... of Roath in the County of Glamorgan ... to receive and obey WHEREAS David Rosser a Rogue and Vagabond was apprehended in the parish of St. John the Baptist aforesaid as a Rogue and Vagabond, (videlicet) by Griffith William [the parish overseer], wandering and begging there ... and upon Examination of the said David Rosser taken before us upon Oath (which Examination is hereunto annexed) it doth appear that he the s[ai]d David Rosser was last Legally settled in the s[ai]d parish of Roath ...*

These are therefore to require you the said Constable ... to Convey the said David Rosser ... to the s[ai]d parish of Roath ... together with this Pass, and the Duplicate of the Examination of the said David Rosser, taking his Receipt for the same ... And you the said Church-Warden—or Overseer of the Poor, ... are hereby required to receive the said Person and provide for him as aforesaid. Given under my Hand and Seal this 25th Day of June in the Year of our Lord 1759.

[signed and sealed by] *HEN[RY] YEOMANS*
THOS. EDWARDS'

(**Q/S R** 1759D 15).

The Examination of John Price —
a Rogue and a vagabond taken on oath before
me Richard Jenkins one of his Majesty's Justices
of ye peace in and for ye said County the second day
of January in ye tenth year of ye Reign of our Lord
George the third of Great Britain France and Ireland
King &c —

Who saith on his oath that he was Born in the
parish of Hentton in ye County of Hereford and
that when he was about ten years of age he went from
there to London and was Bound there to be an apprentice
to one Edward Williams a Silver Smith in ye parish of
Mary Bone near Hanover Square for ye space of seven
years and from thence he shiped himself on Board
the venice Captn Harison for ye West Indies and
were taken in their passage by a French man of war
and were carid to Haverdegrace and was prisoner
there for three weeks, then he got his reprive
and got an Employment there in a foundry for five years
and saith he went from Haverdegrace as
a passenger to Saint Kitts on Board the leak Hull
capt Williams and from thence in ye same ship to
Portsmouth and from thence he saith he came
to Ross in Herefordshire about May in ye year 1765 and
since he saith he hath travelled the County of Pembroke
Carmarthen and Glamorgan and was Employed in casting
of Iron and Brass and making of fishing netts and
that he did beg on ye second and third days of this Instant
in ye parish of Margam in ye said County of Glamorgan
and saith nothing further —

and signed the day
above wr Hen befomeme

Rich Jenkins

The Mark of

John ⟨X⟩ Price

24 *Margam.* The examination of John Price, found begging, 1770.

25 John Lumley, one of Lord Nelson's seamen, watercolour by George Delamotte, *c.*1819.

These Removal Orders were issued by the Justices of the Peace in large numbers; the example quoted above consists of a printed form, in which the names, places, dates and other details have been filled in by the Justices' clerk. The parishes of St. John Baptist, Cardiff, and Roath were contiguous, so that David Rosser was handed over directly by one parish authority to the other. But the printed form shows that, if the pauper had to be conveyed a considerable distance from the parish in which he was arrested to his parish of settlement, then he was handed over by one parish constable to another '*in the next Precinct thro' which he ought to pass in the direct Way to the said parish*' and so on until he reached his destination.

The Order was carried out by the parish constables, who gave receipts for the paupers handed over to them—

'*June 25th 1759 Rec[eiv]ed of Griffith William one of the Overseers of the poor of the parish of St. John the Baptist in the town of Cardiff the Body of the within vagrant by virtue of the within pass*

As witness my hand the Day and year above written
X The mark of Ja[me]s James: petty
Con[sta]ble of Roath'

The receipt is endorsed—'*David Rosser a Vagrant to be passed to Roath*'.
(**Q/S R** 1759D 15).

The Settlement Acts of 1662 and 1696/97 (14 Car. II c. 12, and 8 & 9 Wm. & Mary c. 30) however provided that poor persons might enter any parish if they brought with them from their parish of settlement a Settlement Certificate, guaranteeing to receive them back again if they became a charge upon the poor rate. Parishes must have been reluctant to give such certificates, but did do so from time to time, as is shown by the following order made by Glamorgan Quarter Sessions in July 1724—

'*Ordered ... that a Certificate (bearing date the first day of June Last past) from the Churchwardens And Overseers of the poor of the parish of Whitechurch in the said County Directed to the Churchwardens and overseers of the poor of the p[ar]ish of Radyr in the said County And allowed by S[i]r George Howell Kn[igh]t and Wm. Richards Esq. two of his Ma[jes]tys Justices of the peace for the said County whereby the said Churchwardens and overseers of the poor of the said p[ar]ish of Whitechurch did Certifie that Wm. Edwards, Weaver, and Catherine his wife were Legall Inhabitants of the said p[ar]ish be Rec[eiv]ed by the said Overseers of the poor of the said p[ar]ish of Radyr so that the said Wm. Edwards and Catherine his said wife might Inhabit within the said p[ar]ish of Radyr without Interruption. And it is further Ordered that the Order made by Roger Powell Esq., one of his Ma[jes]ty's Justices of the peace for the said County for Conveying of the said Wm. Edwards to the house of Correct[i]on be discharged upon the said Wm. Edwards paying the said Overseers of the poor of the s[ai]d p[ar]ish of Radyr the Summe of Five shillings towards the Expence of the s[ai]d Order.*'
(**Q/S M** vol. 1, pp. 139, 140).

Before the Settlement Act of 1794/95 Vestries had, and exercised, power to expel from their parishes strangers who came in from outside. On 15th February 1775 the Llantrisant Vestry resolved to apply to the magistrate for a warrant requiring all 'Foreigners' in the parish to declare on oath their parishes of settlement; they were to be sent back there if they could not produce a settlement certificate. (**Llantrisant Vestry minute book**, p. 14). Without such a certificate, a newcomer might find it difficult to find somewhere to live—

'Aberavon. March 14th 1788. At a Vestry held on this Day we whose Names are Under Written being the Majority Present Passed the following Order and Agreed as follows: Viz.—that any Propriot[or] or Occupiers of House or Houses Withing this Town and Parish shall [not] from this Day hence Let any house to any Person or Persons whatever Unless he is a Parishioner or bring a Certificate of his or their Parish.'
The order was signed by the Portreeve, the two Churchwardens, the Overseers of the Poor and five other parishioners.
(**Aberavon Vestry minute book**, f. 39).

Poverty and unemployment were widespread in Ireland in the eighteenth century, so that large numbers of Irish vagrants came into Glamorgan, for example through the port of Swansea. In Irish law there was no such thing as a place of settlement, so that Irish vagrants were sent back under the Vagrancy Acts. A Justice's order of 1759 shows what happened to a poor Irishwoman arrested as a vagrant in Swansea—

'County of Glamorgan. To the High Constables of the Hundred of
Swansea in the County Aforesaid
WHEREAS Margaret Carty a rogue and Vagabond was apprehended in the Town of Swansea in the said County, and upon her Examination taken in writing the Tenth day of June last before me one of his Majestys Justices of the Peace in and for the said County, did upon her oath, swear that the place of her legal settlement was in the City of Cork in the Kingdom of Ireland—and thereupon Benjamin Rees, one of the Constables of the Town of Swansea aforesaid, was order'd by warrant under my hand and seal to convey the said vagrant to the Mumbles in the said County and there to deliver her to Phillip Jeffreys master of the ship called the Prince of Orange then lying there and bound to the said City of Cork, but he the said Phillip Jeffreys refusing to receive the said Margaret Carty and to transport her according to the Statute in that Case made and provided—whereby the said vagrant was return'd to Swansea aforesaid and the said Benjamin Rees was obliged to convey her a second time to the Mumbles aforesaid, and on the Twentieth Day of June last he did there deliver her to John Prance, master of the Francis, bound to Cork aforesaid, who gave him his receipt for the said Vagrant and for the sum of five shillings for her Passage to Ireland—and whereas the said Benjamin Rees did likewise expend and disburse the sum of Two shillings in Conveying the said Margaret Carty twice to the Mumbles aforesaid and Two shillings and six pence for a Boat to carry her off from thence to the ship in the road as verified upon oath of the said Benjamin Rees before me—You the said High Constables are therefore to pay the said Benjamin Rees the aforesaid sum of Nine shillings and sixpence taking his receipt for the same on the back of this Certificate and the same will be

Whereas Margaret Carty a rogue and Vagabond was apprehended in the Town of Swansea in the said County and upon her Examination taken in writing the Tenth day of June last before me one of his Majesty's Justices of the Peace in and for the said County Did upon her Oath swear that the place of her legal settlement was in the City of Cork in the Kingdom of Ireland and thereupon Benjamin Rees one of the Constables of the Town of Swansea aforesaid was order'd by warrant under my hand and seal to convey the said Vagrant to the Mumbles in the said County and there to deliver her to Phillip Jeffreys master of the ship called the Prince of Orange then lying there and bound to the said City of Cork, but he the said Phillip Jeffreys refusing to receive the said Margaret Carty and to transport her according to the Statute in that Case made and provided — whereby the said Vagrant was return'd to Swansea aforesaid and the said Benjamin Rees was oblig'd to convey her a second time to the Mumbles aforesaid, and on the Twentieth Day of June last he did there deliver her to John Prance master of the Francis bound to Cork aforesaid, who gave him his receipt for the said Vagrant and for the sum of five shillings for her Passage to Ireland — and whereas the said Benjamin Rees Did likewise expend and disburse the sum of Two shillings in Conveying the said Margaret Carty twice to the Mumbles aforesaid and Two shillings and six pence for a Boat to carry her off from thence to the ship in the Road as verified upon Oath of the said Benjamin Rees before me — You the said High Constables are therefore to pay the said Benjamin Rees the aforesaid sum of Nine shillings and six pence taking his receipt for the same on the back of this Certificate and the same will be allowed to you by the Treasurer of the County when you pass your Accounts and deliver up this Certificate and receipt. —

Given under my hand and seal in Swansea the Twenty Ninth day of August One Thousand Seven hundred and fifty ___

J Morris

allowed to you by the Treasurer of the County when you pass your Accounts and deliver up this Certificate and receipt.
GIVEN under my hand and seal in Swansea the Twenty Ninth day of August One Thousand Seven hundred and fifty Nine.

[signed and sealed] *JO[HN] MORRIS'*
(**Q/S R** 1759D 5).

Parishes naturally objected to the expense of maintaining paupers and their families who were brought to them by the officers of other parishes. The pauper himself had no right of appeal against the Justice's removal order, but the parish had, and frequently exercised it at Quarter Sessions. It has been said that such appeals took up a large part of the time of that Court from 1688 until 1832. A typical appeal was heard by Quarter Sessions on 11th April 1738—
'*Newcastle. Upon ye Motion of Mr. Nathaniel Taynton an Appeal is Entered from an Order made by Reynold Deere Esq. for ye Relief of Robert Thomas a poor Inhabitant in the Upper Hamlet of ye parish of Newcastle in ye s[ai]d County, And the Merits of the said Appeal coming on to be heard and Determined, And upon hearing what could be Alledged by the Attorneys on both sides, It is ordered By This Court That the Overseers of the Poor of the s[ai]d Upper Hamlet of the s[ai]d parish of Newcastle [pay Robert Thomas] the sume of One Shilling and Six Pence a week for and towards his Maintenance, and It is further Ordered by this Court that the s[ai]d Robert Thomas Live and Reside within the s[ai]d Hamlet and that he also wears the Badge Ordered by Act of Parliament, together with the Costs of this Order.*'
(**Q/S M** vol. 1, p. 363).

The cost of these appeals in legal fees and expenses was considerable, as the following bill shows; the total national sum expended out of the poor rates must have been enormous.
'*Epiphany Q[uarte]r Sess[ions] 1779*
The Inhabitants of Bedwas ag[ain]st The Inhabitants of Lanwonno.
Respondents Bill for Taxation
[£. s d]

	£	s	d
Paid for a Warrant to convence Pauper to swear his Parish		1	0
Officer's Attendance for such Purpose		1	0
Paid Constable for ex[ecu]ting Warrant		1	0
Paid for Pauper's Oath as to his Settlement		1	0
Paid Justices for an Order of Removal and Copy		4	6
Officer's Journey with Pauper to Bedwas with the Order of Removal.		5	0
Paid for Appearance 2s., fee 4s.		6	0
S[ub]p[oe]na Fiat and Fee for Witnesses		7	6
Three Cop[ie]s of S[ub]p[oe]na & Service		6	0
Gave with Copies		3	0
Two Advocates Fees upon appeal	1	1	0
Paid for the Expenses of Pauper and others Horsehire and Carrig 3 Days		15	0
Officer's Attendance 3 days at 5s		15	0

◄ **26** *Swansea.* A magistrate orders the High Constable of Swansea to convey Margaret Carty, a rogue and vagabond, back to Ireland, 1759.

Paid for Order of Confirmation 2 6
Paid for Copy thereof to demand Costs 2 6
Service of the Order and delivering a Copy thereof & demanding
    the Costs... 5 0
Summons to tax Costs, Copies & Services...................................... 8 0
Paid for Taxation 4s. Aff[idavit] 4s... 8 0
Drawing Bill of Costs & Copy.. 3 0

                                                 £5 16 0

                 All[owe]d EDWARDS C[lerk of the] P[eace]'

(**Q/S R** 1779A 59).

    It will be noted how the administration of justice depended on the payment of fees; the Justice's clerk and the constable, for example, received no regular salary, and so exacted payment for every legal document engrossed and every official act performed.

27 *Bettws*. A list of those who brought a Settlement Certificate when they moved into the parish, 1746.

CHAPTER EIGHT

The Justices of the Peace and the Administration of the Poor Law. The Jurisdiction of Quarter Sessions

The Justices of the Peace were the mainstay of the local administration of the Old Poor Law, as of so many other aspects of local government. From 1597 onwards the Poor Law Acts required two Justices of the Peace to meet annually in each locality to appoint the Overseers of the Poor, and to pass their accounts (39 Eliz. I c. 3). They examined vagrants arrested by the constable, and women regarding the putative fathers of bastard children; after examination they signed and sealed their statements. They issued warrants for the arrest of offenders and signed orders for the committal of 'incorrigible rogues' (for example, paupers who returned to the parish from which they had been removed) to the House of Correction until the next Quarter Sessions. All orders, for removal of paupers, indentures or agreements for apprenticing pauper children, affiliation orders, and bonds by which men bound themselves to maintain their bastard children, had to be signed and sealed by the Justices.

Four times a year the Justices of the Peace for Glamorgan met in the Court of Quarter Sessions. Much of the Court's time, as has already been said, was taken up with Poor Law matters. It heard cases brought by parishes to compel reluctant relatives to maintain their kin, it made orders for vagrants to be publicly whipped or committed to the House of Correction, and it was responsible for the House of Correction itself. It heard a vast number of appeals brought by parishes against orders made by individual Justices for the removal of paupers to them; the legal costs of these appeals must have swallowed up much of the money raised by the poor rates. In many such cases paupers were ordered to be shunted from one parish to another with indifference and indeed inhumanity, as witness the following appeal relating to the settlement of a recently-bereaved widow and her four children—

'PILE and KENFIGG against NEWTON NOTTAGE Due Notice being proved It is ordered That an Appeal be entered from an order of Edward Thomas and Hopkin Rees Esquires two of his Majestys Justices of the peace for this County dated the 16th day of May last for the Removal of Mary the Widow of the late Richard John deceased, Mary their Daughter Aged Thirteen Years, Robert their Son Aged Ten

Years, Jenkin their Son Aged 4 years, and Edward their Son Aged Nine Months or thereabouts, from the Parish of Newton Nottage to the parish of Pile and Kenfigg in the said County. And the Meritts of this Appeal coming on now to be heard and determined by this Court and on hearing what could be alledged by the Attorneys on both sides IT IS ORDERED that the Order of the said Justices be confirmed with Costs And the Overseers of the poor of the Parish of Pile and Kenfigg in the said County of Glamorgan are hereby required in obedience to the said order immediately on the Service of this Order to pay unto the Overseers of the poor of the Parish of Newton Nottage in the said County of Glamorgan the Sum of £7 11s.6d. being the Costs Taxed.'
(**Q/S M** vol. 3, p. 187; heard at Neath in July 1765).

Quarter Sessions also heard appeals against the assessment of the Poor Rate. Industrialists appealed against the assessment of their works without giving too much weight to the consideration that in times of recession their workmen and their dependents would make large demands upon poor relief. In 1798, for example, such an appeal was made in respect of the Cyfarthfa ironworks—

'Easter 1798. To the Churchwardens and Overseers of the Poor of the Parish of Merthyr tidvil in the County of Glamorgan and particularly to the Overseer of the Poor of the hamlet of Gellydege in the said Parish.

This is to give you ... Notice that we shall at the next General Quarter Sessions of the peace to be holden on Tuesday the Seventeenth day of April One Thousand Seven hundred and Ninety Eight at Cowbridge in and for the said County, appeal from a certain Rate or Assessment made ... for the necessary Relief of the poor ... for the hamlet of Gellydege ... being the fourth Quarters rate for the Year One Thousand Seven hundred and Ninety Eight of three shillings in the pound (and which Rate we do hereby give you Notice to produce at the next Sessions on the hearing of the said appeal).

Because the said Rate is partial unfair unequal and unjust in as much as we are improperly rated and also overrated and surcharged for Cyfarthfa Iron Works, Coal Mines, Houses, Mills, Furnaces, Forges and other Buildings and Erections, Machines and Engines thereunto annexed, held, occupied, worked and used for ... the making and manufacturing of Iron now in our possession in the hamlet and parish aforesaid, and which are rated at the Sum of Three thousand pounds in such Rate.

And because the said Rate is enormous and made for the Collection of a greater Sum of Money by far than is actually necessary towards the Relief and necessary Support of the Poor ... within the said hamlet of Gellydege ...

And also Because there are several wilful and glaring omissions in the said Rate for that you have left out and omitted ... the name of Thomas Llewellyn of the hamlet and parish aforesaid and neglected to charge Rate and assess him for a certain part of a field called Cae Pen Twyn otherwise called Cae pen Level situate in the hamlet and parish aforesaid in his possession and occupation and liable to be rated towards the Support of the Poor of the said Hamlet ... at and before the time of making such Rate.

And Because you have omitted and left out of the said Rate and Assessment the Names of Thomas John, Pudler, David Richard John, Pudler, Thomas Treharne, Thomas Edmund, John Owen, Pudler, Richard Owen, Edward Hudson, and John Thomas David, all of the hamlet and parish aforesaid and neglected to charge Rate and assess them for certain other parts of the said Field called Cae Pen Twyn ...

28   An Irishman going to Cork, watercolour by George Delamotte, 1819.

And we do hereby also give you notice that we shall proceed to the trial of the said Appeal at the said Sessions.

And we do hereby also give you ... Notice to produce ... on the trial of the said appeal the several and respective Rates made for the Relief of the Poor of the said Hamlet for the years 1793, 1794, 1795, 1796 and 1797, together with the accounts of Receipts and disbursements of the respective Overseers of the Poor of the said hamlet for those said last mentioned Years.

Dated this Ninth day of April 1798.

> *On Behalf of myself and Partner*
> *Richard Crawshay Esquire*
> [signed] *WATKIN GEORGE'*

(**Q/S R** 1798B 35).

Quarter Sessions also made general regulations for the administration of poor relief in the county; such for example as that made in July 1756 for the conveyance of Irish vagrants back to Ireland, and the scale of allowances payable to parish constables who accompanied them to the nearest seaport, and to shipmasters who conveyed them across the Irish Sea (**Q/S M** vol 2, pp. 154, 155). The Court could also make provision for the maintenance of an individual pauper, as when at the Michaelmas Sessions in 1729 it ordered that '*William Meyrick a Lunatick, now a prisoner in the House of Correct[i]on, be from thence discharged, and that the Ma[ste]r of the House of Correct[i]on Convey and Deliver him to one of the overseers of the poor of the parish of Lantrissent who are to p[ro]vide for and relieve him untill further order be made in this Court to the Contrary*'. (**Q/S M** vol. 1, p. 309).

CHAPTER NINE

Later Developments in the Old Poor Law

A great defect in the Old Poor Law was the lack of any central authority able to make and enforce a clear and consistent policy in the country. Authority was divided between the Vestries and parish officers on the one hand, and the Justices of the Peace, sitting in their localities or in Quarter Sessions, on the other. They were seldom able to agree for long as to how to tackle the growing problem of relieving the poor and destitute. Since the parishes and the townships were left to bear the burden from their own resources, they did their best to reduce it by obtaining removal orders against workers and their families who came in from elsewhere; the sum total of human misery caused by the wholesale shunting of paupers from one parish to another can only be guessed at from the pitiful records of the Old Poor Law. The unenviable fate of paupers in the parish workhouse has already been described. Those paupers who remained outside the workhouse received allowances in money and in kind which were usually quite inadequate. The alarm felt by the authorities at the problems of wandering beggars showed itself from time to time in fierce punishments such as public whipping.

Yet in spite of the inadequacy of outdoor relief, in spite of the bad food and squalid accommodation in the parish workhouse, in spite of the cruel public whippings of men and women whose only crime was poverty, the number of paupers continued to rise during the latter part of the eighteenth century and the first half of the next. The economic effects of the Industrial Revolution, enclosures, poor harvests and high food prices, the Revolutionary and Napoleonic Wars – all contributed to aggravate the problem; the increasing burden of the poor rate was made heavier by unequal and unfair assessments of property.

Vestries, and especially the principal ratepayers, were not unnaturally alarmed by the soaring poor rates. On the 1st of May 1812, for example, the Merthyr Tydfil Vestry met *'for the purpose of considering the Report and recommendation of the Committee appointed by an Order of Vestry ... to consider the Cause of the High Rates & the best means of reducing the same'*. Their appointment of a *'General Overseer'* of the poor at a salary of £130 a year was followed in July 1814 by a Vestry decision that *'The payments to the Poor are to be reduced One fifth from*

henceforth except in Case of Sickness'. Complaints continued during the post-war depression; the Merthyr Tydfil Vestry in February 1816 repeated the complaint *'That the Poor Rates are very high in this Parish, and that the Farmers (from the reduced prices of their Commodities) and several Householders are unable to pay their Taxes'*. It was resolved once again *'to appoint a Committee to devise the best means to reduce the Poor Rates'*. (**Merthyr Tydfil Vestry minute book**, pp. 170, 195, 209). In June 1819 the Aberdare Vestry likewise gave the fall in prices after the Napoleonic Wars as the reason for reducing the rates of money relief. The Vestry *'Resolved that in consequence of the great reduction in the price of provisions, Nich[ola]s Morgan's family's allowance be reduced from 12/- to 10/- per week, and that one eighth part be reduced from all the paupers for the present'*.
(**Aberdare Vestry minute book**, p. 10).

By 1830 the Merthyr Tydfil Vestry found its coffers empty—
'Merthyr Tydfil April 29th 1830 ... It appearing that the funds in the hands of the Collectors being insufficient to meet the demands of the Overseer for the usual purposes of payment of the Paupers, upon Application of the Overseers ... for instruction on what to do under the emergency—Resolved that the matter be specifically entered upon at the next meeting & that regular notice be given for that purpose.

[signed] *ANTHONY HILL, Chairman'*
(**Merthyr Tydfil Vestry minute book**, p. 365).

Industrial depression continued, and lengthened the lists of Merthyr Tydfil parishioners who were in arrear with their poor rates; some were noted as *'insolvent'*, and the numerous *'Furnaces out of blast'* of course paid no rates. At a parish meeting held in Merthyr on 24th April 1831 it was *'Resolved That in consequence of defaulters in payment of Poor & Church Rates not having been heard to show why they do not pay their Arrears, this meeeting is of opinion that the next quarters rate cannot be determined, and that this meeting be adjourned'*.
A despairing minute dated 27th March 1832 records a resolution
'that the sum of £1675 4s.9d. appearing due to the parish of Merthyr Tydfil in the Books has arisen from the confused method of keeping the accounts and from a want of due attention to the interests of the parish by the parishioners themselves and by the officers employed for many years past and that immediate attention be henceforth paid to the collecting such parts of this balance as may still be due and capable of being collected and that such part as is really irrecoverable be posted to a separate Folio as irrecoverable'.
(**Merthyr Tydfil Vestry minute book**, pp. 373, 381, 406, 438).

Parishes made desperate but unco-ordinated efforts to lighten the burden. In May 1810, for example, the Llantrisant parish Vestry handed over responsibility for its paupers to two contractors, the Reverend Richard Prichard of Collena [a house about 4 miles NNW. of Llantrisant town, shown on the 1799 map of Glamorgan by Yates] and Howell Harris of Trevorhuge [Treferig, a farmhouse about 3 miles NW. of Llantrisant; shown by Yates]. They were to be paid a sum equivalent to a quarterly rate of seven shillings in the pound, and were also to have *'the benefit of the said poor's People's work, labour and service'*. But by the end of the year numerous complaints from the Llantrisant paupers had been recorded. Jennet William, for example, *'complains that she has had no fire in her*

house this fortnight ago and she owes 2/6 for coal, and will not be trusted with any more until she pays the 2/6. the Rain comes into her Room, and on her bed, she was promised a shift and a pettycoat by the Revd. Mr. Prichard and she never had them, she has no Victuals in her House this day, she was allowed a sack of Coal by the Vestry and was refused by David Arthur'. There followed a dispute between the parish and the contractors, and the arrangement was discontinued.
(**Llantrisant Vestry minute book**, pp. 381-83, 390-92, 393).

On one occasion at least male paupers were billetted on a female pauper. In December 1802 '*At the adjournement of the ... Vestry held at the Bear in the Town of Lantrissent ... it is unanimously agreed ... to support the Paupers as follows viz.—It is Order'd that Howell David late of Pont Clown* [Pontyclun, see Llantrisant parish tithe apportionment, no. 876] *& Thomas Harry, Paupers of this Parish is by Order to Inhabit with Mary Colerake of this Town a Pauper & to have Bed & Bedding & in case she refuses not to be supported by the said Parish*'.
(**Llantrisant Vestry minute book**, p. 275).

It was not unusual for a Vestry to board out a pauper with a parishioner for an agreed sum—
'*May 9th 1812. At a Vestry Duly Publish heald by the inhabitants of the Hamlet of Cwmdu, it is Unanimously Agreed by the said inhabitants of One Part and Rees Hopkin of the same hamlet of the Other Part to Keep and maintain John Rees Pauper from the 9th of May 1812 to the 9th of May 1813 being the space of One Year for Eleven Pounds Ten shillings, and the said Hamlet to find him sufficient Cloathing during the term ...*' This annual agreement was renewed in 1815, though the rate had then been reduced to £8 10s. (**Llangynwyd, hamlet of Cwmdu, Overseers' account book**, pp. 35, 57).

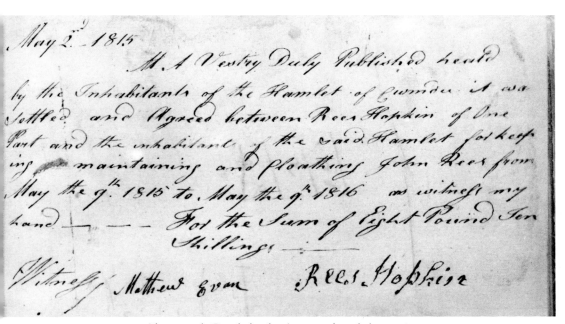

29 *Llangynwyd, Cwmdu hamlet. A pauper boarded out, 1815.*

30 *Llangynwyd, Cwmdu.* The 'Roundsman system', 1811.

Another common arrangement was the 'Roundsman system', by which a pauper was to be lodged and fed by all the ratepayers of the parish in turn— '*Nov[embe]r 1st 1811. It is Unanimously Agreed by the Inhabitants of Cwmdu that Elizabeth Mathew is to be sent Alternately to Every Inhabitants House and to be kept there so many Days as so many Pounds his Valuation is, and Each and Every Inhabitant that will so keep Her shall be paid out of the Poors rate 6d. p[er] day.*' (**Llangynwyd, hamlet of Cwmdu, Overseers' account book**, p. 29).

Gilbert's Act had in 1782 provided that able-bodied persons who could not get work were to be found employment by the parish, and , if necessary, were to have their wages supplemented from the poor rate (22 Geo. III c. 83 s. 32). These provisions were certainly adopted in some Glamorgan parishes—

'*At Vestry buplised* [published] *and held this 8th day of January 1817 in the Vicar[a]ge House of Landilotalybont, we the Churchwarden and the oversier of the poor and the prinsibal Inhabitants of the said parish Do settle and agree To ... Relief David Thomas of 5s. and also To settle David Thomas To work with John David of Talyvan for one week and continue with the parish[i]oners, also the same day we settle To David Thomas his To have 8d. per day and 2s. Relief To his wife, also the same day we settle and agree to but* [put] *Morgan Rees with Thomas Clement of Gwenlais-ycha for Eight pence per day also Relief Morgan Rees of 5s. also the same day we Do settle John David of Pentyn with William Morgan of Castelldy To work for [?] Five weeks at 8d. per day & also we Do Relief John David his Doughter of 1s. per week untill further order ... and also every Inhabitant of the said parish is To keep Every one of the above Named persons three day[s] To every £20 Rent to work.*'
(Llandeilo Talybont Vestry minute book, p. 227).

As time went on, it became common practice for parishes to put paupers to work on the roads, and to supplement their earnings. For example, at a Llancarfan Vestry held on 2nd February 1832 it was '*unanimously Agreed that such able Persons as will seek i[m]ployment with the Surveyor of the road, are to be employed in rotation with the Farmers and others according to every Person's Charge of rate, according to the rate of threepence in the Pound. Wages at 8s. p[e]r week*'.

Later in the same year Llancarfan Vestry agreed on a scheme of family allowances for men engaged upon such work—

'At a vestry held this 13th day of September 1832, it is agreed that all persons who shall seek for work on the road within the parish of Lancarvan shall receive payment for their work as follows—Viz. That every man having a wife shall recieve the sum of five shillings per week and sixpence per week for every child if any, being under seven year old, & every single man shall recieve 3s/6d. per week - hours of Labour being from eight in the forenoon to four in the afternoon, and all persons neglecting to spend the time specified at their work will be reduced accordingly.'

(**Llancarfan Vestry minute book**, pp. 43, 53).

A few years later the Llanrhidian Vestry was ordering an able-bodied pauper to be employed in stone-breaking—

'At a Vestry held at Llanrhidian on the 26th day of January 1835 in pursuance of Public Notice thereof given at the Parish Church of Llanrhidian on the Sunday preeceding— It was resolved that John Thomas Claiming & belonging to this Parish —That for some years past employ'd in Swansea and elsewhere should be employ'd to break Stones for the roads by Measure or weight at the rate generally given by the Turnpike Trustees and that he shall apply for such employment to Mr. Philip Long of Newton and Mr. Wm. Evans of Prisk Overseers of the roads.'

(**Llanrhidian Vestry minute book**, p. 9).

In some cases the Vestry sought to shift the burden of paying such paupers on to another public body—

'Merthyr Tydfil 9 December 1831 ... A Parish Meeting will be held at the Vestry Room on Thursday morning next at eleven o clock for the purpose of taking into consideration the propriety of appointing a person to inspect the paupers who are employed on the parish roads to decide how the said paupers are to be paid and whether any of them are to be [paid] by the Board of Health.'

(**Merthyr Tydfil Vestry minute book**, p. 427).

The French Revolutionary and Napoleonic Wars naturally increased the burdens upon the parishes. The account of the Overseer of the Poor for Llandeilo Talybont records the payment of *'Bounty Money and charges laid out for a Landsman Volunteer to serve in his Majestys Navy for the parish of Landilotalybont ... £18.0.6'.*

(**Llandeilo Talybont Overseers' account book**, 1773-1810, p. 178).

Parishes were also required to supply their quota of men for the Army of Reserve and the Supplementary Militia. The Churchwardens and the Overseers of the Poor would however pay a bounty to substitutes undertaking to perform military service in place of parishioners who could themselves offer money in lieu.

'August 23d 1803. At a Vestry held this Day [in Merthyr Tydfil] according to publick notice giving in Church on Sunday last to settle what Bounty to give to Substitutes for going to the Army of reserve and the Supplementary Militia. It was agreed that it shall be at the discression of the Churchwardens & Overseers of the Poor to Pay each Substitute for the Army Reserve the Sum of Thirty Gu[i]neas if they cant be

obtained for a less Sum and also that it shall be at their discression to Pay Twenty Guineas for each substitute w[hi]ch may be wanting for the Supplemental Militia and they use their utmost endeavours to procure Men on the Above Rates for as many as may be wanting to supply the places of those who have Paid their fines—with the utmost dispatch Possible.'

On 8th November 1804, the same Vestry ordered the Overseers of the Poor *'to pay Lewis Jones of Blaencannaid the Sum of Twenty Pounds being the Sum due to him from the Parish for finding a Man to serve in the Army of Reserve which was to be paid him by James Tranter; but now it is settled for the parish to recover the said sum from James Tranter. The Overseers are Ordered to pay Twenty Pounds to Daniel Williams of the Hamlet of Gellidege for the man that he procured to the Army of Reserve. The Church-Wardens and Overseers are Ordered to call upon James Tranter for the Balance in his Hands and if he does not come to a Settlement to pay four or five pounds a mounth they are to cause him to be arrested'.* (**Merthyr Tydfil Vestry minute book**, pp. 68, 81).

Many men called up in this way left their wives and children destitute and chargeable to their parish of settlement—
'At a Vestry Regularly Published and held this 17th Day of December 1799 in the Vicaridge house of Landilotalybont We the Churchwarden, Overseers of the poor and others of the principal Inhabitants of the said Parish ... do order our Overseers not to Relieve the Militia Mens Wifes and families [of the 8s. p[e]r week—interlined] until satisfaction shall be given to the said parish for their Reimbursement. Also the same Day we do order one of our Overseers or some other Principal Inhabitant to send to Ireland for the Affidavid of the legal settlement of the Militiamen belonging to the said parish.'
(**Llandeilo Talybont Vestry minute book**, p. 129).

The responsibility of the parish for the families of such militia men called up for military service was later defined by Parliament. An Act of 1803 (43 Geo. III c. 47) obliged the parish to give their wives and children a weekly allowance equal to the current wage for one day's agricultural labour, which was not to be less than one shilling.

In some cases parishes sought to relieve themselves of this recurring liability by paying out of parish funds part of the bounty required to buy men out of the army—
'January 27th 1809. At a Vestry held this day [in Merthyr Tydfil] *... Mr. John Owen of Cardiff having sent a Letter to inform Mr. Crawshay that a person is willing to go to the Militia for 20£ instead of Walter Williams a Substitute in the Militia for this Parish, who has a Wife and three Children and they have 6/- a Week from this Parish. Having considered the above proposal Thos. Jones is Ordered to write to Mr. John Owen to agree with the man, on condition that the wife of Walter Williams will pay five pounds towards getting her husband from the Militia.'*

In August of the next year the same Vestry *'agreed to give the wife of Wm. Thomas the Sum of Six pounds towards getting her Husband from the Militia or to live with her husband for one year without having any more allowance from the parish for that time'.* (**Merthyr Tydfil Vestry minute book**, pp. 123, 140).

The maintenance of such men who became prisoners of war was also a responsibility of their parishes. In 1808 the Llandeilo Talybont Vestry resolved that '*We ... Do Settle and Agre[e] to Relife the Briches Brisoners in france* [? at Bitche, an isolated fortress, some eighty miles east of Verdun, according to Edward Fraser on p. 89 of his **Napoleon the Gaoler** (Methuen, 1914)] *of four pound of the parish of Landiotalybont And Also we settle this Money to be Paid of the poor Rate. And Also we Set[t]le Morgan Morgan our Overseer of the poor to pay Griffith Philliph our Churchwarden the Above Sum*'.

(**Llandeilo Talybont Vestry minute book**, p. 179).

During the eighteenth century the numbers of paupers increased, and the responsibilities of the parish officers became ever more burdensome. Some parishes solved the problem by delegating the duties of the Churchwardens and Overseers of the Poor to the Vestry Clerk, who was of course a paid official. In August 1806, for example, the Llantrisant Vestry

'*agreed that John Mathew of the Bear in[n] in Lantrissent to continue for the Present Quarter to be a Vestry Clerk and a Clerk to the several Overseers of the poor in the said parish at the same salary as the Last Quarter and the said John Mathew is to Collect all Rates Pay the Paupers and Relieve the Poor of the said Parish and to attend the said Business in the said Parish and to be accountable for all the moneys in his hand during the said term. But in Case the said John Matthew shall be Oblidged to Travel out of the said Parish on Parish is Business he is to be allowed the resonable expences whatsoever bisnes he may be at in so doing*'.

(**Llantrisant Vestry minute book**, p. 318).

It was found to be more efficient to supervise such paid officials by a small committee which met regularly. So it was that the Llantrisant parish handed over responsibility for poor relief to a Select Vestry –

'*At a Parish Meeting held this 2nd Day of Nov[embe]r 1808 at the Bear Inn in the Town of Lantrissent ... We the Churchwarden and the Overseers of the Poor and the Parishioners assembled ... order that the Overseers of the Poor Call a Vestry on Next Wednesday in their respective Hamlets for the purpose of Electing two proper substantial men within their hamlet to direct & Manage the affairs of the Parish together with* the Minister Churchwardens & overseers of the Poor. This Present Vestry to be adjourned till the 16th Day of this present Month for the purpose of receiving some proposals to be then made respecting the management of the affairs of the Parish.'

At the adjourned Vestry Meeting it was reported that the Select Vestrymen had been duly elected—

'*Whereas the Revd. Richard Prichard and Mr. John Thomas of the Hamlet of Trane Mr. Robert Thomas & Evan Morgan of the Hamlet of Castella, Mr. Thos. Hopkin & David Evan of the Hamlet of Miskin, Mr. Evan Thomas & Howell Morgan of the united Hamlets of Gelliwion and the Town of Lantrissent have been elected by their respective Hamlet as a Select Vestry to Manage & direct the affairs of this Parish Now it is resolved at a Vestry held this 16 Day of November 1808 at the Cross keys in the Town of Lantrissent ... that the Election of the aforesaid Persons for the Above purpose be hereby fully confirm'd and it is further resolv'd that the s[ai]d Vestry Men in conjunction with the Minister, Churchwardens & Overseers of the Poor be considered from this Day to the time the present Overseers deliver in their Account as having all the power of the Parish Vestry transferred to them. That five of the said Vestry Men assembled together pursuant to Notice, together with as Many of the Churchwardens & Overseers as chuse to attend be fully Competent to act. That the attendance of the Minister be optional.'*

(**Llantrisant Vestry minute book**, pp. 344, 345).

Until 1819 the appointment of such Select Vestries required in law the lengthy and expensive procedures of a private Act of Parliament. But in that year a Poor Relief Act, known as Sturges Bourne's Act (59 Geo. III c. 12, ss. 1, 7) gave general powers for parishes to do so, and to appoint salaried Overseers of the Poor. Merthyr Tydfil was one of the first Glamorgan parishes to adopt the Act—

'*Jany. 25th 1822. At a Vestry held this day ... Resolved ... That it is highly expedient to appoint a Select Vestry according to the act of Parliament for that pupose & that the following Gentlemen be unanimously elected ... to act as such ...* [signed] *WM. CRAWSHAY JR. Chairman'*

(**Merthyr Tydfil Vestry minute book**, p.264).

The ironmasters William Crawshay, Josiah John Guest and Anthony Hill, and their agents, naturally figured prominently amongst those elected (**Merthyr Tydfil Vestry minute book**, p. 265). Llandaff followed suit in 1828. Parish meetings were subsequently held every year in both parishes to elect the Select Vestries (**Merthyr Tydfil Vestry minute book**, pp. 267, 271, 272, 391, etc.; **Llandaff parish book**, P/53/41).

In 1804 Parliament, alarmed by the rapidly increasing burden of the poor rates, required every parish in England and Wales to make returns '*relative to the Expence and Maintenance of the Poor in England*' (43 Geo. III c. 144). The total for Glamorgan parishes for the year ending Easter 1803 was £27,780 6s. 2½d., of which £1,168 12s. 9d. was expended in '*Suits of Law, removal of Paupers, and Expences of Overseers and Other Officers*'. During the year 2,000 paupers had received out-relief, and 151 in-relief; 607 of these were not parishioners of the parish where they were relieved.

(printed **Poor Returns**, pp. 692, 693; GRO, R/71).

CHAPTER TEN

The New Poor Law
The Poor Law Amendment Act 1834

All these expedients failed to check the rising tide of pauperism. The Old Poor Law needed to be reformed root and branch; this radical reform came about with the passing by Grey and the Whig Reform Ministry of the Poor Law Amendment Act in 1834 (**Act**, 4 & 5 Will. IV c. 76).

The Act was designed to end the autonomy of the parishes, which had produced such a bewildering variety of practice. A strong central authority was established to put into effect a new national policy of poor relief in a uniform and consistent manner—

'Whereas it is expedient to alter and amend the laws relating to the relief of poor persons in England and Wales ... Be it therefore enacted ... that it shall be lawful for His Majesty ... to appoint three fit persons to be commissioners to carry this Act into execution...' (Section 1).

'And ... the said commissioners shall be styled "The Poor Law Commissioners for England and Wales"...' (Section 2).

'And ... from and after the passing of this Act the administration of relief to the poor throughout England and Wales ... shall be subject to the direction and control of the said commissioners, and ... the said commissioners ... are hereby authorised ... to make and issue all such rules, orders and regulations for the management of the poor, for the government of workhouses and the education of the children therein, and for the management of parish poor children ... and the superintending ... of the houses wherein such poor children are kept ... and for the apprenticing the children of poor persons, and for the guidance and control of all guardians, vestries and parish officers, so far as relates to the management or relief of the poor, and the keeping, examining, auditing and allowing of accounts ... or to any expenditure for the relief of the poor.' (Section 15).

To reduce the enormous numbers of persons receiving 'outdoor' relief, and the consequent burden of the poor rate, the Act proposed the construction of a national system of workhouses, where conditions were to be less tolerable than those of the lowest-paid worker in employment; when these were ready, paupers were to be compelled to enter them—

'And ... it shall be lawful for the said commissioners ... with the consent of a majority of the rate-payers and owners of property entitled to vote ... in any parish ... to order and direct the overseers or guardians of any parish or union not having a workhouse ... to

build a workhouse...' (Section 23).

For greater efficiency, parishes were to be grouped into Unions—
'And ... it shall be lawful for the said commissioners by order ... to declare so many parishes as they may think fit to be united for the administration of the law for the relief of the poor, and such parishes shall thereupon be deemed a union for such purposes, and thereupon the workhouse or workhouses of such parishes shall be for their common use ... but notwithstanding ... each of the said parishes shall be separately chargeable with and liable to defray the expence of its own poor, whether relieved in or out of any such workhouse.' (Section 26).

The ancient parishes of Glamorgan were grouped in 1836 into five Unions—Neath, Swansea, Bridgend and Cowbridge, Merthyr Tydfil and Cardiff.

The practice of making up labourers' wages out of the poor rate had added greatly to the burden upon the ratepayers. The Poor Law Commissioners were empowered in 1834 to make regulations designed to reduce these burdens, pending the construction of Union workhouses able to accommodate the growing armies of paupers—

'And whereas a practice has obtained of giving relief to persons or their families who, at the time of applying for or receiving such relief, were wholly or partially in the employment of individuals ... And whereas difficulty may arise in case any immediate and universal remedy is attempted to be applied ... Be it further enacted that ... it shall be lawful for the said commissioners, by such rules, orders or regulations as they may think fit, to declare to what extent and for what period the relief to be given to able-bodied persons or to their families in any particular parish or union may be administered out of the workhouse of such parish or union, by payments in money, or with food or clothing in kind, or partly in kind and partly in money, and in what proportions, to what persons or class of persons, at what times and places, on what conditions, and in what manner such out-door relief may be afforded.' (Section 52).

The Old Poor Law had been unsystematic and even chaotic, but parish Vestries often displayed humanity towards paupers who must have been known personally to them as members of a small community. The principal inhabitants of the parishes in many instances recorded in the pre-1834 Vestry minutes showed their acceptance of responsibility for fellow-parishioners less fortunate than themselves. The Act of 1834, however, ushered in a new era—depersonalised, aiming at systematic efficiency and economy. The New Poor Law created the dreaded Union Workhouse. The title of Guardians of the Poor acquired an ironic significance; they were so unpopular amongst the Merthyr ironworkers that Sir John Guest's chairmanship of the Board was a significant hazard to his Parliamentary ambitions. [See my *Parliamentary History of Glamorgan* (Christopher Davies, 1978), pp. 49, 162]. But that is another story. After 1834 the parish records from which extracts have been drawn no longer provide such vivid illustrations of 'the short and simple annals of the poor'.

APPENDIX I

Ancient parishes of Glamorgan, arranged under Hundred divisions.

Caerphilly Hundred
Eglwysilan; Gelligaer; Llanfabon; Llanfedw (hamlet of the Monmouthshire parish of Michaelston-y-Vedw); Merthyr Tydfil; Rudry; Whitchurch.

Cowbridge Hundred
Cowbridge; Eglwys Brewis; Flemingston; Gileston; Llanblethian; Llandough-juxta-Cowbridge; Llanharan; Llanharry; Llanilid; Llanmaes; Llanmihangel; Llansannor; Llantwit Major; Llysworney; Pendoylan; St. Athan; St. Hilary; St. Mary Church; Welsh St. Donat's; Ystradowen.

Dinas Powis Hundred
Barry; Bonvilston; Cadoxton-juxta-Barry; Cogan; Lavernock; Leckwith; Llancarfan; Llandough-juxta-Penarth; Llanilltern; Llantrithyd; Merthyr Dyfan; Michaelston-le-Pit; Michaelston-super-Ely; Penarth; Penmark; Peterston-super-Ely; Porthkerry; St. Andrew's Major; St. Bride's-super-Ely; St. Fagans; St. George's-super-Ely; St. Lythan's; St. Nicholas; Sully; Wenvoe.

Kibbor Hundred
Caerau; Lisvane; Llandaff; Llanedeyrn; Llanishen; Roath.

Llangyfelach Hundred
Llangiwg; Llangyfelach; Llansamlet.

Miskin Hundred
Aberdare; Llantrisant; Llantwit Fardre; Llanwonno; Pentyrch, Radyr; Ystradyfodwg.

Neath Hundred
Aberavon; Baglan; Briton Ferry; Cadoxton-juxta-Neath; Cilybebyll; Glyncorrwg; Llantwit-juxta-Neath; Michaelston-super-Avon; Neath.

Newcastle Hundred
Bettws; Coity; Coychurch; Kenfig; Laleston; Llangynwyd; Margam; Newcastle; Newton Nottage; Pencoed (hamlet of Coychurch); Peterston-super-Montem; Pyle; St. Bride's Minor; Tythegston.

Ogmore Hundred
  Colwinston; Ewenny; Llandow; Llandyfodwg; Llangan; Llangeinor;
  Marcross; Merthyr Mawr; Monknash; Penlline; St. Andrew's Minor;
  St. Bride's Major; St. Donat's; St. Mary Hill; Wick; Ynysawdre (hamlet of
  St. Bride's Minor).

Swansea Hundred
  Bishopston; Cheriton; Ilston; Knelston; Llanddewi; Llandeilo Talybont;
  Llangennith; Llanmadoc; Llanrhidian; Loughor; Nicholaston; Oxwich;
  Oystermouth; Penmaen; Pennard; Penrice; Port Eynon; Reynoldston;
  Rhossili; St. John-juxta-Swansea.

Cardiff Town
  St. John Baptist and St. Mary.

Swansea Town and Franchise
  St. Mary.

APPENDIX 2

List of pre-1834 Glamorgan Parish Poor Law records

[In WGARO indicates that the records are stored in the West Glamorgan Area
Record Office, County Hall, Swansea, where they may be consulted]

Vestry minute books in Glamorgan Record Office

Parish	Period	Reference
Aberavon	1776–1823	P/68/4 (in WGARO)
Aberdare	1819–1843	P/61/5
Cardiff, St. John (1 vol.)	1776–1820	P/122/CW/26
(2 vols.)	1819–1830	P/122/5,6
Colwinston	1825–1876	P/90/CW/2
Cowbridge	1814–1893	P/8/CW/25
Llancarfan	1821–1894	P/36/13
Llandeilo Talybont	1782–1823	P/108/8 (in WGARO)
Llangan	1820–1835	P/95/CW/15
Llangiwg	1799–1815	P/59/CW/42/1,2
(too fragile for production until repaired)		(in WGARO)

Parish	Period	Reference
Llangyfelach (2 vols.)	1784-1802	P/58/CW/36
[minutes of parish		(in WGARO)
meeting incl. rules of the workhouse, lists		
of inmates and inventory of furniture, 1784]		
Parcel Mawr hamlet	1816-1830	P/58/27 (in WGARO)
Llangynwyd (Cwmdu) (1 paper)	1800	P/82/17
Llanishen	1821-1833	P/55/CW/70
Llanrhidian	1833-1894	P/111/3 (in WGARO)
Llansamlet	1818-1876	P/60/CW/69
		(in WGARO)
Llantrisant Vestry minutes	1759-1772,	P/62/3
and accounts (3 papers)	1781	
Vestry minute books	1771-1802	P/62/4
[originally one volume,	pp. 1-270	
repaired and rebound in	1802-1815	P/62/5
1949 as two; pagination	pp. 271-end	
as one volume]		
Merthyr Tydfil	1799-1833	P/4/2
	1833-1896	P/4/3
Newton Nottage	1818-1883	P/85/3
St. Bride's Major	1774-1817	P/89/CW/8
[includes charity accounts, 1785-94]		
Swansea, St. Mary	1761-1831	P/123/CW/79
		(in WGARO)
Wenvoe	1829-1858	P/51/CW/20
Ystradyfodwg	1750-1777	P/67/3
copy extracts (1 booklet)		

Vestry minute books in the National Library of Wales, Aberystwyth

Parish	Period	Reference
Llangynwyd	1826-1890	
Llansannor	1757, 1785-1789 [included in the parish register for the period 1727-1786]	

Overseers' account books in the Glamorgan Record Office

(Some volumes contain also accounts of Churchwardens, Petty Constables or Highway Surveyors)

Parish	Period	Reference
Baglan	1784-1835	P/69/3 (in WGARO)

Parish	Period	Reference
Bettws	1709-1795	P/77/3
Cardiff, St. John	1711-1731	B/C 2/3
[also list of Poor Law certificates brought into Cardiff, *c*.1750]		
	1830-1837	P/122/7
Cardiff, St. Mary	1739-1760	CL MS 5.113
Cogan	1802-1810	P/32/11
Coity	1719-1757	P/80/CW/12
	1757-1801	P/80/CW/13
Eglwysilan	1819-1829	P/1/2
Glyncorrwg	1759-1819	P/72/3 (in WGARO)
Llandaff (6 vols.)	1700-1720	P/53/37
	1740-1759	P/53/38
	1759-1777	P/53/39
	1785-1794	P/53/40
	1807-1839	P/53/41
Ely hamlet	1829-1831	P/53/42
Llandeilo Talybont	1773-1810	P/108/7 (in WGARO)
Llangan (2 vols.)	1787-1835	P/95/CW/14,15
Llangeinor (1 paper)	1684-1685	P/96/2
Llangiwg (2 vols.)	1799-1815	P/59/CW/42/1,2
(too fragile for production until repaired)		(in WGARO)
Llangyfelach, Rhyndwy-clydach hamlet (3 vols.)	1809-1894	P/58/4-6 (in WGARO)
Llangynwyd, Cwmdu	1809-1820	P/82/13
hamlet (2 vols.)	1820-1837	P/82/14
Llanharan	1832-1836	P/15/2
Llanilltern	1797-1816	CL MS 5.77
Llanishen	1713-1715	D/D X 318/2
	1790-1825	P/55/CW/74,75
Llanmaes (2 papers)	1637-1638	Merthyr Mawr Estate D/D N 240/1,2
Llansannor	1817-1819	P/20/1
	1827-1830	P/20/3
Llantrisant (4 vols.)	1814-1837	P/62/28-31

Parish	Period	Reference
Llantwit Fardre (1 paper)	1679	CL MS 4.1108
(4 vols.)	1736-1786	P/63/1
	1787-1815	P/63/2
	1815-1836	P/63/4,5
Llysworney	1774-1785	P/22/2
Margam (1 paper) (fragile and partly illegible)	1799	P/83/3/2 (in WGARO)
Merthyr Mawr	1768-1813	P/99/CW/25
	1810-1837	P/99/CW/47
Neath	1673-1674, 1689-1700	P/76/1 (**NB** in GRO)
Penmark	1738-1762, 1769, 1780-1797, 1801	Fonmon Castle Estate D/D F vol. 79
Pentyrch (2 vols.)	1821-1837	P/65/1, 2
Peterston-super-Ely	1772-1800	P/48/1
Radyr	1740-1795	P/66/CW/16
St. Athan	1785-1831	P/7/CW/4
St. Bride's Major	1821-1831	P/89/10
St. George's-super-Ely [included in register with copies of settlement certificates, 1702, 1703]	1703	P/34/CW/3
	1818-1830	P/34/CW/6
St. Hilary	1728-1821	P/12/3
St. Mary Hill	1739-1740, 1778-1817	P/98/CW/9
St. Nicholas	1800-1837	P/45/CW/14,15
Swansea, St. Mary (Town and Franchise) House of Industry, and outdoor and casual relief (17 vols.)	1821-1833	P123/1-17 (all Swansea vols. in WGARO)
Wenvoe	1804-1836	P/51/1
Ystradowen (2 vols.)	1785-1827	P/26/1
	1826-1895	P/26/2
Ystradyfodwg [included in parish register]	1735-1750	P67/CW/1
(3 vols.)	1750-1835	P/67/CW/89-91

Overseers' account book in the National Library of Wales

Parish	Period	Reference
Llansannor	1748-1791	
[included in the parish register for the period 1727-1786]		

Other Poor Law documents for Glamorgan parishes in the Glamorgan Record Office (including accounts of Swansea House of Industry)

Parish	Document	Period	Reference
Bishopston (1 paper)	Apprenticeship Indenture	1764	P/103/1 (in WGARO)
Colwinston (1 paper)	Settlement Certificate	1751	P/90/4
Ewenny (1 paper)	Settlement Order	1699	P/92/1
Leckwith (2 papers)	Bastardy Bonds	1794	P/40/3,4
Llancarfan (1 paper)	Bastardy Bond	1745	P/36/1
(1 paper)	Justice's Order to Constable to apprehend father of bastard child	1780	P/36/2
(2 papers)	Removal Orders	1801, 1815	P/36/3, 4
(1 paper)	Pauper's Deposition	1799	P/36/5
(1 paper)	Apprenticeship Indenture	1790	P/36/6
(13 papers) (some fragmentary and fragile)	Settlement papers, Removal Orders Bastardy Order and Deposition	1767-1808	P/36/38,39
Llangynwyd (72 papers) (photocopies)	Bastardy Bonds and other Bonds to maintain paupers, an Order of Filiation, Removal Orders, Paupers' Depositions, Settlement Certificates	1737-1842	P/82/29/1-43
Llantrisant (1 paper)	Workhouse rules	1784	CL MS 6.13
(1 paper)	Warrant to apprehend the father of a bastard child	1834	P/62/76
Merthyr Mawr (11 papers)	Correspondence concerning payment of relief to a pauper and his wife	1830-1835	P/99/CW/49

Parish	Document	Period	Reference
Neath (11 papers)	Settlement papers and Bonds	1689-1696, 1774, 1781	P/76/5
(3 papers)	Apprenticeship Indentures	1721, 1738, 1758	P/76/4
(1 paper)	Order from Chief Constable to Petty Constables to list freeeholders from which Justices will select Overseers of the Poor	1789	P/76/8 (**NB** all in GRO)
Peterston-super-Ely	Bastardy Bond	1810	P/48/2
St. Bride's Major	Removal Order	1828	P/89/8
St. George's-super-Ely	Bastardy Deposition	1806	P/34/1
Whitchurch (2 parchments)	Poor Rate Assessments	1778, 1809	P/6/101, 102
(1 paper)	Apprenticeship Indenture	1822	P/6/115
Wick (5 papers)	Depositions and Removal Order	1788-1830	P/102/CW/9-12
(1 paper)	Apprenticeship Indenture	1770	P/102/CW/13
(5 papers)	Bastardy Bonds	1780-1809	P/102/CW/14-18
Ystradowen (5 papers)	Bastardy Bonds	1793-1813	P/26/5
Ystradyfodwg (1 paper)	Bastardy Bond	1805	P/67/CW/92

Maps

Tithe Maps

The Glamorgan Archive Service holds a complete set of tithe maps, with their accompanying apportionments, surveyed parish by parish, by professional surveyors in the 1840's, following the Tithe Commutation Act of 1836.

Those for West Glamorgan parishes are housed in the West Glamorgan Area Record Office in County Hall, Swansea; the others are at the Glamorgan Record Office, County Hall, Cathays Park, Cardiff.

These plans were originally the parish copies and kept in the parish chest. The National Library of Wales, Aberystwyth, also holds a set of tithe plans and apportionments, which were originally the bishop's diocesan copies.

Some plans may give incomplete information for those parts of a parish which were in the ownership of a landlord who had already agreed to compound his tithe payments. No tithe plans were made for Briton Ferry or Margam.

Yates, 1799

A facsimile reproduction of the map of Glamorgan surveyed by George Yates can be consulted in the GRO and WGARO, and copies are available for sale.

Ordnance Survey

Photocopies of the unpublished manuscript maps surveyed during the period 1811-1813 and drawn on a 2-inch to the mile scale can be consulted in the GRO, WGARO or NLW.

Parish boundaries

A map showing ancient parishes in Glamorgan can be consulted in the GRO and WGARO.

Occasionally lost documents are recovered and reach the Record Office, so additions may be made to this list in the future. The Glamorgan Archive Service would be grateful for any assistance or information which might lead to the recovery of further documents which have survived. Each additional item will extend our knowledge of the inhabitants of Glamorgan in the past.

INDEX TO SUBJECTS

Figures in **bold** refer to illustrations

work outside Quarter Sessions, 57
  appoint overseer, 37, 41, 57
  apprenticing, 16-19, **7**
  approving especial relief, 47
  issuing Orders, Warrants, 11-13, 14, 31-2,
    37, 39, 49-55, 57, 61, **26**
  passing overseers' accounts, 57
  taking examinations, 11-12, 48-9, 57, **2**,
    24
  signing documents, ix, 57
  see also Quorum

L

lace making, female children 'bound' to, 21
latrine, 35, 43, **18**
legal proceedings
  costs, 39, 57, 69
  to compel overseer to serve, 41
lime, 35
literacy, viii, 2, 44
lunacy, 23, 43, 60, **12**
  Bethlem hospital, London, 23, **12**

M

magistrate *see* Justice of the Peace
maintenance, 10-15, 23, 33, 60, 63-4, **29, 30**
  Bond, 11
  Order, 10-11
measure (grain), Cowbridge, 7
medical care, 23-7, 44
  apothecary appointed to workhouse, 27, **13**
  doctor, **8**, **10**
  midwife, 15
  sea-water cure, 23-7
  spa water cure, 27
  surgeon appointed to workhouse, 27, 44, **13**
  wine, **10**
mental illness *see* lunacy
militiamen, 66-8
  bought out by parish, 67
  bounty to volunteers, 66-7
  dependants, 67-8
  prisoners of war, 68
  substitutes, 66-7
milk, *see under* food
mill assessed for rates, 3
minister (clergyman)
  administer benefactions, 6-7
  announce vestry meetings, 2
  approve workhouse diet, 44
  attendance at select vestry, 69
  payment for burial, 39, **19**
  workhouse trustee, 44
money, ix
  see also relief

N

Napoleonic Wars, 61-2, 66
  prisoners of war, 68
navy
  bounty money for volunteer, 66
  'pressed' into, **2**
  service in, 48-9, **2, 24, 25**

O

oakum picking, **9**
occupations
  apothecary, ix, 27, **13**
  attorney, 10, 39, 55
  basket maker, **9**
  bellman, crier, 2
  blacksmith, **27**
  brass caster, **24**
  carpenter, 28, **27**
  carrier, 29-30
  clergyman, 12, 47, 62, 69
  collier, 12
  cook, 8, **5**
  cooper, 33, **15**
  dairymaid, 17
  doctor, [8], **10**
  farmer, 2, 15, 16, 37, 44, 62, 65
  farm labourer, 16
  glazier, 35, **18**
  gaoler, 30, 35, **18**
  innkeeper *see* victualler
  ironmaster, 4, 71
  iron caster, **24**
  labourer, 8, 9, 12, 13
  lace maker, 21
  landowner, 44
  lexicographer, viii
  mariner, 10, 23, 48-9, 53, 60, 66, **2, 24, 25, 26**
  merchant, 49, **2**
  midwife, 15
  militiaman *see* soldier
  musician, **1, 28**
  net maker, **24**
  oakum picker, **9**
  officer of excise, **4**
  pedler (without licence), 49, **2**
  puddler, 58
  road mender, 66
  seaman *see* mariner
  sailor *see* mariner
  servant, domestic, 16, 19, **7**
  silversmith, **24**
  soldier, 10, 66-8
  spinner, 29
  stone breaker, 66
  surgeon, 27, 44, **13**

INDEX TO PERSONAL NAMES

Figures in **bold** refer to illustrations

The personal names in the index are supplemented by details of status, occupation, office held and parish. The appelation 'Mr.' was an indication of status and has been retained in the index. The individual would probably have described himself as a 'gent.', above a yeoman but below an esquire.

ABBREVIATIONS

chw.—churchwarden
con.—constable
esq.—esquire
gent.—gentleman
jun.—junior
JP—Justice of the Peace
lab.—labourer

ov.—overseer
sen.—senior
spr.—spinster
vict.—victualler, innkeeper
wid.—widow
yeo.—yeoman

Elizabeth, 29
John, 16-17
John, vict., 23, **12**
Lewis, 23, **12**
Mathew, **29**
Phillip, **10**
Sara, pauper, 39, **19**
Thomas, pauper apprentice, 20, **8**
William, 17
Evans, Ann, 11, 23
Mr. Azariah, ov., Llancarfan, 16-17
Mr. John, chw., Llancarfan, 16-17
Mr. Watkin, surgeon & apothecary, 27, 44, **13**
Mr. William of Prisk, highway surveyor, Llanrhidian, 66
Eustance, Howell, 8

F

Foster, John, ov., Gelliwion hamlet, Llantrisant, 41
Frances, Mary, 44
Rachel, sister of Mary, 44

G

George, Watkin, 60
Gibbs, John, benefactor, 6
Giles, John, jun., 15
Glascott, William, ov., Town hamlet, Llantrisant, 42
Gordon, Mary, vagrant, 33, **15**
Gregory, Philip, ov., Neath, **7**
Griffice, John, gent., **4**
Walter, gent., **4**
Griffith, Ann, 23
John, **13**
Thomas, ov., Miskin hamlet, Llantrisant, 39
Guest, Sir Josiah John, ironmaster, 69
Chairman of Vestry, 4
Chairman of Board of Guardians, 71

H

Harison, captain of the *Venice*, **24**
Harris, Howell of Treferig, Llantrisant, 62
Harry, George, son of, **20**
Thomas, pauper, 63
Hary, William, 35, **18**
Hill, Anthony, ironmaster, 4, 69
Chairman of Vestry, 62
Hopkin, Rees, 63, **29, 30**
Mr. Thomas of Miskin hamlet, Llantrisant, 69
Hopkins, John, gent., **4**
John, **12**
Richard, son of, 27

Howel, John, ov., Llandeilo Talybont, 14
Howell, Sir George, knight, JP, 52
Richard, **23**
Thomas, **4, 30**
Howells, Mary, 42
Hudson, Edward, 58
Hugh, Jno., vict., 28
Humphreys, Mr. William, attorney, 10
Hutton, Jno., blacksmith, **27**

J

Jacob, James, vestry clerk and chw., Llantrisant, 41
James, James, con., Roath, 52
Thomas, 41-2
Jeffreys, Philip, master of the *Prince of Orange*, 53, **26**
Jenkin, Evan, pauper, **20**
Gwenllian, spr., 12-14, **6**
Thomas, of Rhubridwell, Llantrisant, 23, **12**
Jenkins, Evan, 8
Mr. Griffith, chw., 9
John, 8
John, gent., officer of excise, **4**
Richard, esq., JP, 32, **24**
Thomas, idiot daughter of, 23
John, Ann, 39, **19**
Catherine, grand-daughter of Robert, 11
David, lab., 12
David, pauper, 16
David Richard, puddler, 58
Edward, son of Mary, wid., 58
Gwenlian, **10**
Jenkin, son of Mary, wid., 58
Joseph, 44-6, **23**
Lewis, 41
Margret, *alias* Mary Lewis, wid., vagrant, 31-2
Mary, wid. of Richard and children, 57-8
Mary, pauper, 11
Mary, daughter of Mary, wid., 57-8
Philip, benefactor, 6
Rees, son of Robert, 10-11
Rees, grandson of Robert, 11
Richard, 57
Robert, 10-11
Robert, son of Mary, wid., 57-8
Thomas, puddler, 58
Thomas, **13**
William, grandson of Robert, 11
William, of the George inn, Llantrisant, 41
Johnson, Dr. [Samuel], lexicographer, viii
Jones, Elizabeth, 29
Mr. Evan, 44
Evan, nephew of John Jones, 42
Jenkin, 35, **18**

Jenkin, chw., Neath, **7**
John, 41-2, **12**
Lewis, of Blaencannaid, Merthyr Tydfil, 67
Margaret, apprentice, 16-17
Mary, *alias* Gordon, *alias* Murray, vagrant, 33, **15**
Phillip, basket maker, **9**
Thomas, 67
William, ov., Llandeilo Talybont, 34
William, wine cooper, 33, **15**

L

Lewellin, Edmund, **8**
Richard, ov., Llysworney, **8**
Lewis, Charles, **7**
Evan, ov., Bettws, **4**
Mary, wid., vagrant, 31
Mary, **17**
Richard, carpenter, **27**
Thomas, *alias* Tom Marlborough, **11**
William, chief constable, Newcastle Hundred, 37
Leyshon, Alice, **10**
Leyson, William, **4**
Leysone, Lewis, **4**
Llewelin, Jno., carpenter, **27**
Llewellin, John, JP, 17
Llewellyn, Thomas, of Gellideg, Merthyr Tydfil, 58
Long, Mr. Philip, of Newton, highway surveyor, Llanrhidian, 66
Loyd, Richard, **17**
Lumley, John, seaman, **25**

M

Maddocks, Anthony, of Cefn Idfa, Llangynwyd, gent., **4**
Mansel (Mansell) family of Margam, 8, **5**
Marlborough, Tom, **11**
Mathew, David, poor-house keeper, 47, **22**
Elizabeth, pauper, 64, **30**
Evan, ov., Ystradowen, 39, **19**
John, of the Bear inn, Llantrisant, vestry clerk and clerk to overseers, 68
Matthews, Eleanor of Aberaman, Aberdare, benefactor, 6
Meyrick, William, lunatic, 60
Miles, Thomas Harry, 30
Montague, James, 21
Morgan, Catherine (Kate) of Neath, wid., 19, **7**
Edward, benefactor, 8
Elizabeth, **20**
Evan, of Castella hamlet, Llantrisant, 69
Francis, ov., Llancarfan, 12

Howell, of Gelliwion and Town hamlets, Llantrisant, 69
John, ov., Llansannor, **21**
Jno., **17**
Martha, 23
Morgan, ov., Llandeilo Talybont, 68
Morgan, of Pencefnarda, Llandeilo Talybont, **22**
Nicholas, 62
Rees, con., Llandeilo Talybont, 14
Mr. Thomas, gaoler, 30
Thomas, **8**
Mr. William, attorney, 10
William, of Castelldy, Llandeilo Talybont, 65
Morris, John, JP, 55, **26**
Murray, Mary, vagrant, 33, **15**

N

Nelson, [Horatio], Lord, **25**
Nichol, Jenat, 39, **19**
Nicholl, Illtid, benefactor, 4
Nicholas, Thomas, and wife, 46

O

Owen, Mr. John, of Cardiff, 67
John, puddler, 58
Mary, 23
Richard, 58

P

Parry, Rev. John, JP, 11-12
Pemberton, Joseph, merchant, Philadelphia, 49, **2**
Penry, Mary, **20**
Phillip, Evan John, **8**
Griffith, 39
Philliph, Griffith, chw., Llandeilo Talybont, 68
Picton, Rev. Edward, JP, 12-14, **6**
Popkin(s), John, of Talygarn, esq., 44, **23**
Powell, Anthony, esq., **4**
Catherine, benefactor, 9
Edward, **21**
Gabriel, JP, 48-9, **2**
Mr. [? Gabriel], **17**
Gervas, 9
Roger, JP, 52
Prance, John, master of the *Francis*, 53, **26**
Preece, Margaret, 35, **18**
Price, John, vagrant, 49, **24**
Captain John, benefactor, 9
Prichard, Rev. Richard of Collenna, Llantrisant, 62-3, 69
Proby, captain of the *New Thunder*, 49, **2**
Pryce, M., JP, **7**

INDEX TO PLACES

Arranged under parishes

Figures in **bold** refer to illustrations

NOTES